SHIFT
COMMERCIAL

HOW TOP COMMERCIAL BROKERS
TACKLE TOUGH TIMES

HOW TOP COMMERCIAL BROKERS
TACKLE TOUGH TIMES

SHIFT
COMMERCIAL

BUDDY NORMAN
WITH JAY PAPASAN

3 4 5 6 7 8 9 DOC

ISBN: 978-1-932649-20-8

This publication is designed to provide accurate and authoritative information in regard to the subject matter covered. It is sold with the understanding that neither the author nor the publisher is engaged in rendering legal, accounting, or other professional service. If legal advice or other expert assistance is required, the services of a competent professional person should be sought.

—From a Declaration of Principles jointly adopted by a Committee of the American Bar Association and a Committee of Publishers.

Smooth seas do not make skillful sailors.

PROVERB

ACKNOWLEDGMENTS

Writing a book is rarely the result of an individual's effort but rather the efforts of many ... *SHIFT Commercial* is definitely the latter. First, I would like to thank Gary Keller for allowing me to be a part of his *New York Times* bestselling Millionaire Real Estate series. This book is a commercial adaptation of the discerning tactics and business strategies for residential agents that Gary shared in *The New York Times*, *Wall Street Journal*, and *USA Today* national bestseller *SHIFT: How Top Real Estate Agents Tackle Tough Times*.

I also want to thank Mark Willis, Mary Tennant, and Mo Anderson for encouraging and supporting me and KW Commercial while this book was being developed. Bryon Ellington and Jim Talbot also provided crucial leadership and support throughout the process. Very special thanks are owed to my dedicated staff at KW Commercial—Cory Older, Schuyler Williamson, and Gloria Sivori—for allowing me the time to commit to the book while continuing to build North America's fastest-growing commercial real estate brokerage firm.

Honestly, I probably wouldn't have been in a position to write this book without the advice and counsel of two of my most important commercial real estate mentors: Roger Staubach and Kevin Hayes. Both provided crucial coaching and support when I was building and developing my commercial real estate career. They showed me how to do this business at a high level with complete integrity in everything they did—the "high road" might well be named in their honor.

A special thanks to the 43 members of the Commercial Leadership Council (CLC) of KW Commercial that shared their collective 800 years of commercial real estate expertise with me and whose tactics and stories hopefully make the book relevant, inspiring and results oriented for the reader. The CLC includes the following individuals: Page Aiken, John Aucamp, JB Bader, Andrew Barnes, OJ Bobek, Barry Bounds, Daron Campbell, Kristan Cole, Larry Culbertson, Brock Danielson, Dale Donovan, Jennice Doty, Kyle Drake, Charles Frankel, Ron Fredette, Blair Gilbert, Michelle Rich Goode, Graig Griffin, Mark Hughes, Charlie Kennedy, Matt Klein, Larry Kueser, Nancy Lemas, Charlie Lockwood, Jim McClung, David Neault, Ann Page, Jeffrey Peldon, Winston Penny, John Powell, Matthew Rasche, Chris Sands, Joe Scripa, Jim Solnes, Joe Sosky, Robert Tufts, David Vercher, Butch West, Rhonda West, Geoff Wilkinson, Joe Williams, Ken Wimberly, and Paul White.

In addition to our CLC, the following real estate and commercial professionals also donated their time and wisdom to this effort: Michael Balson, Cliff Bogart, Mark Bratton, Jeremy Cyrier, Tom Daves, Tony DiCello, Reagan Dixon, Darrow Fiedler, Jon D. Greenlee, Dan Henderson, Vikki Keyser, Ben Kinney, Dianna Kokoszka, Len May, Charles "Mac" McClure, Steven McMurtrie, Ray Meglio, Scott Miller, Eric Nesbitt, Christopher Perez, Peter Pessetto, and Mark Raccuia.

I'd be remiss if I didn't thank the amazing production, sales, and marketing teams that helped us turn a bunch of words on paper into a bona fide book, fit to be sold. On the production side, Tamara Hurwitz and her team of Mary Keith Trawick, Jennifer Boyd, Maryanne Jordan, and Jeffrey Ryder made sure our i's were dotted and our t's were crossed. Tom Freireich, Anthony Azar, and Danny Thompson have been and will continue to be great champions for the book to both our clients and our strategic partners—thanks guys! And thanks to the design and marketing team led by Ellen Marks, that includes the super-talented Annie Switt and Michael Balistreri, for making the book look great and making sure commercial brokers hear about it.

On the writing side, thanks to Barbara Opyt for assisting us with the initial interviews and research in the early drafting process. Special thanks to Lari Bishop, senior editor with Greenleaf Book Group, who helped me and my coauthor Jay Papasan take unrefined ideas, concepts, and interviews and craft them into the final drafts of the book. I would also like to offer special thanks to Jay for his significant guidance and direction in the writing of *SHIFT Commercial*. His probing insight and unique writing skills can take a mundane subject and make it an insightful and entertaining read. I trust you will enjoy the book as well as profit from its advice.

Finally, thanks to my wife Jeanne and my children Forrest, Sarah, and Hannah for tolerating the long days and nights at work ... I love you very much.

CONTENTS

FOREWORD

Fresh out of college in 1979 and just months into my real estate career, I immediately got my first taste of a real estate shift.

On the heels of the energy crisis, interest rates soared as high as 18 percent. As you can imagine, sales ground to a halt. I kept at it, writing four or five offers every month, but nothing would close. Things looked bleak when I went home for Christmas, having not closed a sale in almost five months. My mom suggested I get a part-time job at 7-Eleven, which I politely declined. I was confident that I was doing the right things and would eventually make it. My dad offered to loan me some money to get me through, but he didn't just write a check.

"How do I even know you've been working?" he asked. I ran out to my yellow Volkswagen Beetle and retrieved my "database." My database was in fact a 3 x 9 index-card box: my contacts organized A to Z in one half and the other half divided into twelve months with follow-up notes for all my leads and contacts. It may sound primitive, but not only was this state of the art in the pre-personal computer age, but it was also extremely effective. I sat down with my dad and walked him through my lead management system. I showed him all the leads I had in my pipeline and what I was doing and would be doing to turn those leads into closed business. After a moment's consideration, he replied, "I'll bet $500 on that box."

Within weeks I closed an out-of-town buyer and paid my dad back. I regained my footing, went on to hit all my financial goals, and became one of the top salespeople in my firm that year.

A key distinction should be made between my challenges in the final months of 1979 and my successful 1980. After the shift, I dove into learning the fundamentals of the business. I met daily with a scripting partner and dedicated myself to mastering the language of closing for appointments and making sales presentations. I worked my lead generation plan and called and called and called. The one thing I saw quickly was that a shifted market is like a headwind and you must lean into it and work harder to make progress. Luckily, I was new enough not to realize that it was taking extraordinary effort to achieve even average results. Selling a home where the seller had to pay 12 discount points was just business as usual for a 22-year-old rookie like me. Without knowing it, I was learning the invaluable lessons of how to build a business when little business is being done.

In 1987, it happened again. Changes to the federal income tax code wrought havoc in the market and, seemingly overnight, the population of our Board of Realtors® dropped from more than 5,000 to less than 2,000. This time I knew better. I recognized the shift for what it was and what it would require. The lessons I'd learned in my first shift helped me make critical adjustments to my game plan: work smarter, as well as harder. At the time, I was building a new real estate company, and I not only had to lead myself through the shift but also the agents I worked with. Together, we adapted to the new reality and creatively worked hard to grow through the crisis. In the end, we came out on top: the number one firm in our market by any measure—a title we've never relinquished.

Real estate is cyclical ... but we forget. The good times spawn a collective amnesia until the next shift comes along to remind us that selling real estate demands the most from its career practitioners. Those who learn to recognize these shifts and adjust their mindset and action stand to emerge as market survivors and sometimes as market leaders as well.

In 2000, in the aftermath of yet another financial meltdown—the infamous dot-com bust—we created a training seminar called Shifting Markets to better prepare our associates for a tough buyers' market, where sellers cling to the past and buyers fear what lies ahead. Then, in 2006, it was no real surprise to learn that agents in our company were calling in and asking for the Shifting Markets manuals. The first murmurs of what is now called the Great Recession had been echoing since the previous fall and agents everywhere were looking for clues to how to weather the storm. Markets that had previously been some of the hottest were the first and, often, hardest hit. Sign calls were down. Inquiries nonexistent. Buyers backed out of contracts ... Another shift began, one which we now see as the greatest economic shift since the Great Depression.

So we began to focus our research on top agents who weren't just surviving but thriving in these tough times. That research culminated in the 2008 publication of *SHIFT: How Top Real Estate Agents Tackle Tough Times,* which went on to become a *New York Times, Wall Street Journal,* and *USA Today* national bestseller, as well as a series of seminars that attracted more than 30,000 attendees across North America.

Today, we look up and the real estate shift is following a now familiar course. As it has in the past and will most certainly in the future, a shift moves through the residential market to collide with the commercial market. As residential roofs multiply, a wave of commercial expansion typically follows in its wake. And the same is true when those same houses sit unsold and unoccupied or when they fold to foreclosure and face vacancy and neglect: commercial goes into retreat. And the brokers who lease and sell these properties face challenges that just a few years ago seemed unimaginable. They are looking for answers. *How do I navigate this market? How can I first get my business back to profitability and, in turn, find opportunity here?*

With *SHIFT Commercial,* our goal is to share lessons from commercial brokers who are finding uncommon success in the midst of a historic and uncommon recession. While this book can be read as a stand-alone piece, it can also be seen as an extension of *SHIFT.* I sincerely hope you'll take the time to read it as well, since most of the tactics featured in the original work are equally effective in the commercial arena. That said, the commercial real estate business is unique. Commercial brokers have unique customers, distinctive challenges, and novel solutions. The goal of this book is to highlight those differences while acknowledging, despite many claims to the contrary, that there is much common ground as well. As with *SHIFT*, it's our intention that the commercial tactics in this book be as timeless as they are timely. So whether you're reading this book in the wake of our current shift or a decade from now when the next one is coming around the bend, the rules of the game won't have changed. Even if your current market is booming, the same game plan that will lift your business in a tough market can make it soar in a less challenging one. No matter the reason, when you want to shift your business to another gear, the strategies are always the same. The fundamentals, as we wrote in *SHIFT*, never go out of style.

For *SHIFT Commercial*, we partnered with commercial veteran Buddy Norman. For the past two and a half years, despite a shifted market of historic proportions, Buddy has been building the fastest-growing commercial brokerage firm in North America. With more than twenty years of commercial brokerage experience, Buddy has represented tenants from local entrepreneurs leasing a few thousand square feet to

Fortune 500 clients leasing more than 500,000. He's been on the front lines of the business and achieved extraordinary success through up and down markets. Buddy draws not only from his personal experience as a commercial broker and business owner but also from the more than 800 years of combined commercial real estate experience of his Commercial Leadership Council, a group of more than forty commercial veterans helping to build this new enterprise.

As you turn these pages, hopefully scribbling notes and aha's in the margins, make both a commitment to tackling these challenges with everything you have, as well as a commitment to building newer, stronger habits that will serve you in better times. One-year wonders come and go, but the measure of any professional is how well they weather the lean years. To quote Benjamin Disraeli, "There is no education like adversity." And it is a good teacher. Reservoirs of strength, faith, and ingenuity are rarely revealed in prosperous times. Tough times will strip away the gloss and help you see the latent talents you always possessed.

So if you will learn these lessons now and commit them to habit, you'll join a small class of professionals who actually yearn for tough markets to weed out the uncommitted and allow them to win new customers, market share, profitability—their unfair share of the business. Only when you shift your mindset and your actions can your business truly shift into a higher gear.

Gary Keller
COB and Cofounder of Keller Williams Realty, Inc.
www.kellerink.com
July 25, 2011

INTRODUCTION

Tough times don't last, tough people do.
GREGORY PECK

Real estate shifts are easier to recognize than they are to acknowledge. One day job growth is beginning to stall and, seemingly overnight, vacancies are on the rise. Tenants start asking to downsize. Commercial property valuations level off. Negative news stories feed the worries of buyers and tenants. New development halts. Fear creeps in. Then, the market that was quietly losing ground goes into full retreat as tenant delinquencies turn into owner delinquencies and lenders sever lines of credit. Rents go into a free fall as owners scavenge for income to offset a rising tide of red ink. Deals unravel. Buyers and tenants hunker down to wait for a steal. Bankruptcies mount. Eventually, big commercial real estate owners start selling their companies or simply close their doors. Credit freezes up. Banks begin to shut down ... Sound familiar? If you've been in the business for any length of time, it should. In our experience, this drama plays out roughly once every ten to twelve years.

There are four clear contributors to a downward trend in commercial real estate markets; any two of these can create a shifted market. The post-2007 time period has offered us a perfect storm of all four: excessive valuations, lax loan standards, overbuilding, and economic recession.

Speculation fuels bubbles, and bubbles are defined by valuations that lose touch with reality. These excessive valuations come in two forms: low cap rates and unrealistic income assumptions. When these valuations drive commercial cap rates into the 3 to 5 percent range, you have to ask why any rational investor would risk their capital when they could get the same rate of return on a T-bill. The answer is they wouldn't. But, then again, the run-up to a market shift isn't really defined by rational behavior. Then there are income projections that effectively bail out an otherwise poor purchase decision. "So for the first few years you're building more equity than income, but as rental rates are buoyed by inflation (visualize an Excel chart with rosy rental projections driving up income year after year) the property will really hit its stride ..." The discipline of discounted cash flows gets lost and these speculative pro formas persist long after rental rates are actually in decline. Most find it hard to accept that the experience isn't just a blip and that a whole new reality has dawned.

CAUSES OF A SHIFTED MARKET

Pick Any Two {
1. Excessive Valuations
2. Lax Loan Standards
3. Overbuilding
4. Economic Recession
} **= Shift**

Figure 1

On the flip side of excessive valuations are the lenders who accept them. Appreciating markets can make investors numb to risk and offer the illusion of safety in numbers. The cycle begins with surprise ("Wow, the market is heating up"), then progresses to incredulity ("They paid $_____ for that?"), and eventually the sheer volume of speculative comps gives rise to uncertainty ("Are we being too risk averse?"). This is the moment of truth. In some cases, lenders become vocally indignant ("This is madness!") which is rarely received warmly. After all, they are raining on everyone's parade. Only in hindsight are they seen as courageous. In most cases, lenders uneasily relax their standards ("We've got to adjust to the market ... we're losing too much business to the competition."). The erosion of standards is usually in direct proportion to the length and size of the speculative run-up until, suddenly, the lender's role has reversed: They are no longer serving as a check against speculation—they are unintentionally abetting it.

There is an old saying, "Give a developer money to build a building and he'll build two." Excessive valuation and lax loan standards also allow for speculative development to take place. Overbuilding in segments of the market is the outcome. With the long lag time between ground breaking and ribbon cutting on commercial properties, supply can stealthily outstrip demand and a low inventory sellers' market is transformed into a buyers' market with years of supply. Overbuilding is a deadly recipe for high vacancy rates, lower rental rates, and a slump in property values.

Finally, the fourth major factor is the economy. Just like the commercial and residential real estate markets, the economy has cycles too. Recessions happen—in fact, they are inevitable. Based on data from the National Bureau of Economic Research, the U.S. economy has cycled into recession 33 times between 1854 and 2009, or about every 4.5 years. When unemployment rises, the need for office and industrial space goes down because fewer people are working. And, because fewer people are working, there is less spending and also less demand for retail space. Depending on the depth of the recession, it may affect multifamily properties positively, if people that were previously homeowners suddenly become renters. However, for the most part, recessions are less than benevolent.

This may sound like we're oversimplifying, but please understand this: Shifts aren't complicated. Include any other measure you like, but generally speaking excessive valuations, lax loan standards, overbuilding, and economic recession are the hallmarks of a market shift. Your job as a commercial real estate professional is to be vigilant and watch for signs. If you've ever read Edward Chancellor's excellent work, *Devil Take the Hindmost: A History of Financial Speculation*, you know how this plays out time after time. As the title implies, the last ones to acknowledge the shift are often the hardest hit. So don't be the last, be the first.

The dangerous tendency is to think, "This time is different." It almost never is.

THE TACTICS

The book *SHIFT: How Top Real Estate Agents Tackle Tough Times* presents twelve tactics that residential real estate agents deploy in response to a downturn in the market. Each of these tactics is applicable to the commercial real estate professional as well, so we organized this book in the same way. The twelve tactics are listed in order of priority because we believe that what matters most at any given moment is what should command the majority of your energy and focus.

1. **Get Real, Get Right** – Mindset and Action: You can't control the market but you can control your outlook and your response to it. Get real about the market and get right in your action.

2. **Re-Margin Your Business** – Expense Management: Re-margin your business and get serious about expense management and profitability. Stop spending money "on it" and start investing money "in it."

3. **Do More with Less** – Leverage: Learn to do more with less. Maximize your productivity, upgrade your systems, and top-grade your people.

4. **Find the Motivated** – Lead Generation: Focus your lead generation on finding motivated clients. Master the tasks, skills, and scripts of your lead generation methods. Time-block to ensure this gets done every day.

5. **Get to the Table** – Lead Conversion: Converting leads to appointments to clients is the most dollar-productive thing you can do. Never assume you have a lead until you have an appointment, and never assume you have a client until you have an exclusive representation agreement.

6. **Catch People in Your Web** – Internet Lead Conversion: The Internet is one of the most untapped resources in commercial real estate. Catch people in your Web and focus your Internet strategy on capturing contact information for follow-up and conversion. Everything else about your web presence can be important, but is secondary to this.

7. **Price Tight to the Market** – Shift Pricing Strategies: Master pricing, whether for lease or for sale, so your listings aren't just "on the market," they are "in the market."

8. **Stand Out from the Competition** – Property Staging Strategies: Master strategies that will help your listings stand out from the competition, sell or lease faster, and garner a higher price.

9. **Create Urgency** – Overcoming Buyer and Tenant Reluctance: Help your clients overcome their reluctance and acquire genuine urgency. Timing the market is not an option when you are possibly missing out on the best opportunities today.

10. **Expand the Options** – Creative Financing: Build a creative finance team around you and put this to use whenever you can. Align yourself with those who have money and those who are lending money. Work creatively with sellers, buyers, and lenders to find a way to close the transaction.

11. **Master the Market of the Moment** – Identify and Establish Needed Expertise: Each shift has its own unique opportunities. Markets of the moment in commercial shifts tend to be tenant and landlord leasing representation, Small Business Administration (SBA) qualified buyers, high quality investments, as well as short sales, foreclosures, and REOs.

12. **Bulletproof the Transaction** - Issues and Solutions: Bulletproof your transactions. Assume nothing! Establish client expectations up front, involve yourself in the selection and supervision of vendors, be personally involved in due diligence, inspections, repairs, and any final negotiations.

As a commercial real estate professional, you have only one choice in how to respond: When the market shifts, so must you. It's not unusual to go through a period of denial or disbelief, but any prolonged shift will require you to adjust your tactics to achieve different results or pay the financial price of sticking to your guns. You get to choose. With a little downsizing and rationing, maybe you can ride it out. We prefer to remove the maybe and focus on first surviving and then thriving. How you choose to respond will define your outcomes. As Gary wrote in *SHIFT*, "Success isn't for the chosen few, it's for the few who choose."

TWELVE TACTICS
FOR TOUGH TIMES

#1 Get Real, Get Right – Mindset and Action

#2 Re-Margin Your Business – Expense Management

#3 Do More with Less – Leverage

#4 Find the Motivated – Lead Generation

#5 Get to the Table – Lead Conversion

#6 Catch People in Your Web – Internet Lead Conversion

#7 Price Tight to the Market – Shift Pricing Strategies

#8 Stand Out from the Competition – Property Staging Strategies

#9 Create Urgency – Overcoming Buyer and Tenant Reluctance

#10 Expand the Options – Creative Financing

#11 Master the Market of the Moment – Identify and Establish Needed Expertise

#12 Bulletproof the Transaction – Issues and Solutions

TACTIC #1
GET REAL, GET RIGHT –
MINDSET AND ACTION

Buckle up, we're headed to the bottom of the ninth.

ERNIE HARWELL, HALL OF FAME BASEBALL ANNOUNCER

The story is more than 2,500 years old, but it still has relevance. In Aesop's Fable "Hercules and the Wagoner," a driver hauling a heavy load comes to a muddy place where his wagon wheels sink to the axles in the muck. Seeing this, the wagoner throws down his horse whip and prays to Hercules for help "in this my hour of distress." Hercules appears, but not to lend his mythic muscle to the task. Instead, he gives the wagoner a 650 BC piece of his mind, "Tut, man, don't sprawl there! Get up and put your shoulder to the wheel … Never more pray to me for help until you have done your best to help yourself!" The moral: Help comes to those who help themselves.

Don't judge the driver too quickly. Unless you're truly extraordinary, you've probably been there too. When the wagoner found himself in a bad circumstance, instead of looking for his own solution, he looked for someone to make the problem go away. He looked *outside* instead of *inside*. His reward? A telling off from a mythical Arnold Schwarzenegger type!

We've seen it again and again. When markets shift, brokers practically go through the five stages of grief—denial, anger, bargaining, depression, and acceptance—before they can pick themselves up and get after it again. In our experience, the faster you can move through that process and accept your circumstances, the greater your advantage. The longer you sit and worry about the market or complain about what the banks are or are not doing, the more behind you will be in implementing the tactics in this book that can propel you forward. As the proverb goes, "You can't change the wind; you can, however, adjust your sails."

In short, nothing happens until you acknowledge where you are. *I'm stuck.* Change begins when you own the solution. *Now, what am I going to do about it!* It's a two-step process of mindset and action. First you get real and then you get right.

Don't confuse owning the solution with going it alone. As Gary constantly reminds us, no one succeeds alone—in fact, you will almost certainly need help. Just remember that help begins with self-help. When you are doing all you can, you may even be surprised at the help that will arrive from unexpected quarters. It's human nature. It's a lonely wait for the tow truck for the guy who runs out of gas and calls AAA on his cell. But when a driver is pushing his car down the road, there is clarity and urgency about his need for help, and total strangers will block traffic to lend a hand. "Hey, you steer and I'll push!"

Once you've got your head on straight and you are ready to attack the problem, it becomes imperative that you focus, focus, focus on the basics. Of the many things you could be doing, there are only a vital few you *should be doing.* We believe the twelve tactics identified in this book are the vital few. Chances are you knew them long before you read them here. But if knowing what to do and doing it were easy, the weight loss industry would go belly-up, right? One of the best ways to bridge knowing and doing is urgency. The stark economic reality of a shift can be an immense source of this. A shift narrows your options; sometimes it only gives you one. And, actually, that may be a gift in disguise; when you only have one option, it's no longer a question of identifying what to do. You must simply do.

The tactics that immediatly follow are the most vital and urgent of the few. If you haven't yet done the tough work for remargining your business, that comes next. You can no longer afford to waste a nickel. Hand-in-hand with remargining is the top-grading of people and systems. Both cost you money, either because you've invested poorly in your business or because you're losing revenue to inefficiency or lack of commitment. You can't afford to accept anything less than excellence when you're trying to do more with less. Then, you personally will drive the business by spending the majority of your time and energy on lead generation and lead conversion—what you should have been doing all along! Often forgotten, sometimes abandoned, and rarely respected, the basics are never outdated.

Ultimately, getting real and getting right requires you to make a commitment to personal and professional growth. "Opposition is a natural part of life," writes Stephen R. Covey. "Just as we develop our physical muscles through overcoming opposition—such as lifting weights—we develop our character muscles by overcoming challenges and adversity." This may be the most challenging time in your business life, and what you do now will say volumes about who you are and who you are willing to become.

TACTIC #2
RE-MARGIN YOUR BUSINESS –
EXPENSE MANAGEMENT

Name a business that has been ruined by downsizing. I can't name one.
Name a company that has been ruined by bloat. I can name dozens.
CHARLIE MUNGER, IN *WARREN BUFFETT SPEAKS*

Steven Spielberg's *Jaws* is considered by some to be among the best films ever made and credited by most as the father of the summer blockbuster. So let us be the first to enshrine it as an object lesson in financial management. When Robert Shaw's character, Quint, offers his services to Chief Brody, the mayor, and the Amity city council, he urges, "We gotta do it quick, that'll bring back your tourists, put all your businesses on a payin' basis ... But you've gotta make up your minds. If you want to stay alive, then ante up. If you want to play it cheap, be on welfare the whole winter." The business owners must choose: Pay Quint to kill the shark or face a summer season with no income.

That ominous great white is the shifted market that has effectively closed our beaches. There is no waiting and wishing for circumstances to change. Like the townsfolk of Amity, you have to assume "the shark" isn't going anywhere and make adjustments as if your business depends on it *right now*. Because it does.

When the revenue disappears, as a business owner, you have two choices: Find new business income or make your expenses go away. The former is about lead generation and the latter is about cost cutting. The trap most sales people fall into is to go for the revenue without first (or possibly ever) trimming the fat. It's not surprising: Most chose a career in sales because they know how to find and convert clients—it's a strength. And expense management, for many, is about as attractive as a trip to the dentist. Businesspeople do both and they start with a thorough scrutiny of every expense—fixed or variable—on the P&L. They understand that the cycle of revenue is long—you must find and convert a prospect into a client and then find and close a deal—while the cycle of expenses can just be one phone call away.

In a shift, it's a race to get back into the black. The first brokerage to emerge from the red has an enormous advantage. While your competitors are still fighting to keep the lights on, you can return to investing energy and money in growth. One can never do this too quickly. In commercial real estate, too many months in the red is like a summer without tourists in Amity—quite possibly the downfall of your business.

THREE AREAS YOU MUST ADDRESS:

1. Personal Finances

2. Business Expenses

3. Business Cost of Sales

Figure 2

These are the same areas that every business suffering tough times has to tackle. For six decades, Toyota Motor Corporation was a paragon of profitability. Then, in 2008 and 2009, disaster struck in the form of a collapsing global economy, and Toyota suffered a crushing blow—it couldn't book a profit for its fiscal year. What did the leaders do? Accept that the economy was lousy and there was nothing they could do to generate profit until the economy recovered? No. They developed their "2010 Emergency Profit Improvement Plan." Yes, the plan focused on increasing revenues by identifying motivated buyers (particularly people who wanted hybrids) and expanding into new regions with specialized products. But mostly, the plan focused on cutting costs. They sold a large manufacturing plant and used their other plants more efficiently, they developed workshare programs to reduce labor costs while retaining valuable employees, they improved the efficiency of plant maintenance, they cut back on all employee travel, they streamlined product development to reduce R&D expenses ... The list goes on and on. Against all odds, and despite a massive, costly recall program, in 2010 they booked a profit. And their efforts to streamline their operations will put them ahead of their competitors—who, by the way, have been losing billions—as the economy turns around.

If Toyota can do it, you can do it.

1) PERSONAL FINANCES

For most real estate professionals, the number one expense in their business is their own finances. Not only have they built business expenses—rent, salaries, technology—around pre-shift revenue, they've built their personal lifestyles around it as well. And the pressure to make ends meet, much less balance the books of the business, can be painful.

The knife cuts both ways: While a stressful business life can result in hard times at home, a stressful personal financial life full of worry, doubt, and fear rarely breeds a confident, successful business outlook. And the less energy you spend worrying about paying the bills, the more energy you'll have to convert leads and close business.

Now is the time to meet with your spouse and cut all personal expenses to the bone. Fixed costs like a mortgage and car payments need to be honestly examined. You may need to put the house on the market and downsize. The car may need to be traded in. No question about it, it's time to sell the boat! The vacation home may go too, or at least be placed in the rental pool when not in use. Family vacations may need to become staycations or be done on a budget. Instead of driving the family to the airport, you might be driving to your destination. It is never clearer than in a shift which expenses are required and which are discretionary.

Additionally, your discussions with your spouse should include a review of your liquid investments, cash reserves, and savings balances. You'll need to get on the same page about the potential burn rate of these reserves during the shifted market. Be honest and realistic about your earning potential over the next twelve months and adjust your personal expenses accordingly. For most brokers, it takes six to nine months for their transactions to work their way through the pipeline to closing. After adjusting for higher fallout rates (if historically 25 percent fell through, in a shift as many as 50 percent or more of your transactions may collapse), you should be able to project your approximate net income for the next two to three quarters. Revisit your projections on a regular basis; you will likely have to make adjustments again before you find equilibrium.

Rally the family together, explain what's happened, and ask them all to pitch in. You may be surprised at their willingness to contribute. Lemonade stands probably won't be your answer, but moral support on the home front can be priceless.

And when things turn around, build a fortress around the things you would never ever want to question again. When you talk to entrepreneurs like Gary Keller and Mo Anderson, you'll find they faced similar trials and emerged with a firmer financial foundation to build on. Both emerged from tough times and quickly set goals around owning their personal homes outright. They invested their income so that they would have safe, residual income to pay for the things that mattered most, no matter what happened in the business. In high times, thinking like this is derided as overly cautious and, in tough times, revealed to be financially wise. As you strive for your maximums in your commercial business career, identify the financial minimums you'll be willing to accept along the way, and build a financial moat around them so you can sleep soundly through good times and bad. The commercial real estate business is tough enough (especially in a shift) without the added stress that comes from supporting an excessive or lavish personal lifestyle.

2) BUSINESS EXPENSES

Personal finance leads us straight to business finance. Possibly the most overlooked business expense for most real estate professionals is a personal salary. By and large, brokers ride the tides of revenue, counting on their personal savings instead of business reserves to smooth out the ups and downs. Very few pay themselves a salary at all, much less one that would be in line with what it would cost the business to replace their contributions. If anything, a personal salary is seen as a tax deduction. But this is one of the hard lines between being self-employed and running a true business. So ask yourself the question: Would you rather be a self-employed broker or own a commercial business? We recommend the latter.

A fair salary paid to the owner is invaluable in two ways: First, it identifies the true value of the business—how much the owner can profit if he/she is no longer working in the business. (And, by the way, when that number is zero, you are effectively self-employed!) Second, it serves as an early warning system for shifts. The day you have to consider a salary reduction because the business can't make payroll, you know that re-margining action is required.

COMMERCIAL BUSINESS EXPENSES

1. Salaries/Benefits
   - Your Income
   - Staff Salary
   - Contract Labor
2. Business Development
   - Marketing
   - Prospecting
3. Occupancy (rent, desk fees, etc.)
4. Communication/Technology
5. Education/Dues
6. Transportation
7. Equipment/Furnishing
8. Office Supplies
9. Insurance
10. Professional Services

Figure 3

After examining your personal income and salary, it's time to align the rest of your expenses with your current revenue to make sure there is profit at the end of the day. The bottom line is that you have to manage expenses to ensure that you are always operating from a position of profitability. One of the greatest lies perpetrated on business is "You have to spend money to make money." Experience and research has shown that profits are found and kept through sharp expense management. Businesspeople don't spend—they invest. When you invest, you expect your returns to exceed your investment. We would be better served to say and think, "Cut costs for profit. Invest for growth."

With that maxim in mind, address your P&L and balance sheet with the mindset of a budget bully: No expense is too small to be picked on and picked apart. You will be harshest on any costs that are not directly in the path of revenue.

One of the first things people do with their money is buy back their time. They hire an assistant to do the grunt work and pay for systems to take the sting out of daily chores. So be cognizant of why you've been spending the money. Your personal or executive assistant doesn't have to be laid off, but they may get a new job description more in line with business development or be shared with other commercial brokers in your group. Salaried employees can be converted to hourly ones and, when the situation warrants it, they may even get their compensation in the form of production bonuses (but only if you can truly tie their work to revenue). Service contracts can be terminated or, at worst, renegotiated. Your vendors may not be happy to hear from you, but most would rather accept less than get nothing. These are the same skills you use to help tenants renegotiate leases and owners rework debt payments—put them to use for your own business now.

Kristan Cole, a top commercial broker in Wasilla, Alaska, spends nothing on print advertising and refuses to be caught in the trap of "ego marketing." Print ads declaring years in the business or market share are often defended as brand marketing, but despite their high costs, they can be difficult to trace to direct business leads. The majority of her investment sales and property listings come from her monthly email campaign to a select group of business leaders and owners, a group she refers to as her "Stat Group." She gets the data for free from a title partner, so other than her team's time investment to format and email the report, a vital component of her lead generation is essentially free.

Scrutinize everything. Fixed expenses can be converted to variable expenses and those that can't be eliminated altogether likely can be reduced. If you are using debt to fund your operations, you must recognize that this is a critical issue to address, especially in a market shift when monthly debt service can weigh you down and wear you out. Muhammad Ali once observed, "It isn't the mountains ahead to climb that wear you out, it's the pebble in your shoe." A debt burden that can't be covered by cash flow in the midst of a market shift is no different.

Take a hard look at your technology. For many, technology can evoke more dread than budgeting, so if necessary, call on a team member or friend who has a passion for it to help you look for savings. Your Internet and cell phone providers are not going to unilaterally offer to lower your cost of bandwidth. However, if you shop your Internet and telephone services around, you will find lower costs each and every year. In the last ten years, the IT industry has made a profound shift from the high cost of everyone owning their own software and hardware to the lower-cost "application service provider" model. You may be pleasantly surprised when you look at the IT costs you are currently paying, and what those same services are available for on the Internet.

Technology can also offer cost savings by streamlining core business tasks. Mark Raccuia of Chicago, Illinois, has cut costs dramatically by no longer copying, binding, and sending proposals and packages via overnight mail. He says, "We have automated the development of the packages with professional scanners and electronic document assembly. A package used to take hours to put together and it would weigh 12 lbs., and then we had to ship it overnight at great expense. Now, we use a scanner and create a PDF package that I can send with the touch of a button in thirty seconds." Instead of saying, "I'll send it tomorrow and follow up in a few days," Mark now says, "I'll send it now and call you tomorrow." His business isn't just operating more smoothly, he is saving time and hard-earned money as well.

With hosted services, Dropbox storage, easy website templates, and discounted telephone offerings, you need to reevaluate your IT and communication services at least every three years. If you haven't, you are likely paying too much.

Charles "Mac" McClure,
Dallas, Texas

At the end of the day, you'll find that you're effectively adopting a zero-based budget mentality. Instead of building your current budget with your old one as a starting point, you're taking everything to zero and rebuilding it from scratch. The point of the exercise is that last year's budget holds no financial wisdom for today. It's time to reboot: Hit the restart button and reset your business finances from the ground up. Every expense will need to be justified in light of today's market conditions.

Chances are that many of the investments you made in your business in the past will be immediately revealed as inappropriate today, and that's by design. A good place to start is by asking the zero-based budgeting questions in figure 4. This will help you to focus on investments in the activities, programs, and salaries that are helping you achieve your goals, rather than expenses that are funding perks that are simply nice to have around. We'll talk more about this in Tactic #3, in terms of getting more out of systems and people, and Tactics #4 and #6, in terms of smart investments in lead generation.

What you will likely see from the zero-based budgeting exercise is that you are funding activities and programs that make your life easier but don't necessarily help you to produce revenue. The programs that help you achieve the highest revenues, your business development efforts, should stand out as the best places to invest your money and be clearly strategic at this time. Zero-based budgeting is about helping you make effective investments in your business.

3) BUSINESS COSTS OF SALE

After scouring your personal and professional expenses to remove the deadweight and debris, your next task is to clean up your costs of sale. Even though the lingo is "costs of sale," it also applies to your leasing business as well. For our purposes, costs of sale are costs directly tied to your income—whether that income comes from sales, leases, referrals, or other fees. In most cases, this translates as "If you don't get paid, they don't get paid—it's that simple." Typical costs of sale include commission splits you negotiate with co-brokers and junior brokers; commission splits paid

ZERO-BASED BUDGETING QUESTIONS

Evaluate each and every line item in your budget and ask the following questions:

1. What goals and objectives does this activity/program/salary contribute to?

2. Are these goals and objectives important enough to warrant the expenditures?

3. What would happen if the activity/program/salary was not done at all?

4. Are there other less costly and more effective ways of achieving these objectives?

5. Where would the activity/program/salary fit if all were displayed in order of importance?

6. Would the benefits be greater if the funds spent on the activity/program/salary were used elsewhere?

7. Does this expense have a clear and direct link to revenue?

Figure 4

to team members such as an investment specialist, a tenant rep specialist, or a project leasing specialist; bonuses paid on production; commission-based referral fees paid to other agents; any commission-based fees you pay to your vendors (such as design, architectural, construction, and project management fees); and, less commonly, any base salary paid to full-time brokers on your team. Costs of sale do not include advertising and marketing; those are expenses. While those costs are in the path of your income, they are too far from the source and you will still have to pay them even if the deal doesn't close.

So how much are you spending to close a deal? Look at every sale, every lease commission, every consulting fee earned, and calculate the actual cost of the sale. After you factor in the probability of closing, all of the splits, and all of the costs directly involved in getting that sale, you may find that some avenues of business are simply not returning as much as you thought (see figure 5). This analysis will help you to determine which lines of business are returning the highest benefit, and you may be surprised by what you find. Traditionally, you may have looked for the big payouts on investment sale commissions, but in a shifted market you may find that tenant representation or consulting fees are sources of income that have fewer costs attached. In fact, in a shift, tenant representation is a market of the moment that you can leverage. We'll discuss this opportunity and others in Tactic #11.

When I started in the business, I'd meet with my broker and we would run this kind of analysis on all the business I had in the pipeline at the start of each year and after the second quarter to determine my likely income and, of course, his brokerage income as well. It was required and it was also invaluable for me in my personal and professional budgeting work.

COMPARATIVE COST OF REVENUE PRO FORMA ANALYSIS

1) Investment Sales

Average Gross Commission	$50,000
Probability of Closing This Year	x 33%
Pro Forma Gross Income	$16,500
Expenses	
Deliverables/Marketing	($3,000)
Cost of Sales	
Split to Junior Broker (20%)	($3,300)
Paid Prospecting	
- Annual Cost ($10/hr x 15hrs/wk)	$7,800
- Annual Transactions Developed	÷ 4
- Paid Prospecting Cost/Transaction	($1,950)
Referral Costs	
- Referral Fee (25%)	$4,125
- Referral Probability	x 20%
- Pro Forma Referral Cost	($825)
Subtotal Expenses and Cost of Sales	($9,075)
Subtotal Broker Income	$7,425
Brokerage Split (50%)	($3,713)
Pro Forma Net to Broker	$3,713
Percentage Net	(22.5%)

2) Tenant Representation

Average Gross Commission	$25,000
Probability of Closing This Year	x 90%
Pro Forma Gross Income	$22,500
Expenses	
Deliverables/Marketing	($300)
Cost of Sales	
Split to Junior Broker (20%)	($4,500)
Paid Prospecting	
- Annual Cost ($10/hr x 15hrs/wk)	$7,800
- Annual Transactions Developed	÷ 10
- Paid Prospecting Cost/Transaction	($780)
Referral Costs	
- Referral Fee (25%)	$5,625
- Referral Probability	x 30%
- Pro Forma Referral Cost	($1,688)
Subtotal Expenses and Cost of Sales	($7,268)
Subtotal Broker Income	$15,233
Brokerage Split (50%)	($7,616)
Pro Forma Net to Broker	$7,616
Percentage Net	(33.8%)

Figure 5

Note, the pro formas in the Comparative Cost of Revenue Pro Forma Analysis (above) are based on a traditional brokerage model where negotiated expenses and costs of sale are shared and splits are generally fifty-fifty. They are based on experiences and assume a shifted market. Use these as a guideline, but it's vital you do your own math for all your primary areas of business. If you specialize in leasing, the numbers in the tenant representation example should be in the ballpark, but you'll likely have a lower probability of closing in a shifted market.

Now, once you have a sense of your costs of sale for your primary income sources, you have two choices: 1) Shift your business model to lines of business with higher net, or 2) Find ways to reduce the costs in your current lines of business. Expenses are one thing, but costs of sale almost always translate directly to someone else's income. So while this analysis should illuminate the sources of revenue that have the least economic baggage, it should not be used to renegotiate "I win, you lose" commission splits on everything else. In most cases, the commission splits based purely on a percentage are perfectly reasonable up to a point. However, the higher the commission amount, the more likely it may be that you are overpaying for the service. The solution in these instances is to cap commission splits at a certain level. Negotiations grounded in fairness—they shouldn't have to accept less-than-fair pay and you shouldn't have to pay more than a fair rate—have the greatest chance of working out.

In 1909, the *Galveston Daily News* authored one of the earliest business references to a "sacred cow" when the columnist objected to the idea that raw materials would be unreasonably excluded from tariffs. So the idea of the "untouchable" in business goes a long way back. In the commercial world, brokerage commission splits with their affiliated brokers is just such an untouchable, undiscussable, unthinkable topic. Brokerage com-panies have historically adopted a "take it or leave it" attitude with the house split as well. The truth is that this approach isn't really serving anyone anymore. We'd assert that it is absolutely unreasonable to place something, which for most commercial brokers is their most expensive cost of sale, out of bounds for discussion. If there was ever a time to ask "Am I getting a fair return on my brokerage splits?" it is during a shift! You should also look at fees and other charges: Can some of these brokerage firm infrastructure costs be eliminated or unbundled into pay-as-you-go fees?

Shifts give rise to innovations, and are almost always when new business models emerge to compete with the old. The best brokerages will get this and adjust their value proposition and cost structure accordingly. Make no mistake, we don't advocate for discount brokers or brokerages. In our research and experience, neither is sustainable in the long run. The goal is to determine if the value proposition is being fulfilled and whether you're paying a fair price to get it in a market with many new options.

Charlie Lockwood, managing director of a commercial firm in Atlanta, Georgia, moved his practice because his current brokerage offered more flexibility and "has low operating costs and thus an exceptional broker payout structure." In short, Charlie looked at his options, did the math, and determined the best move for both re-margining his business and having future opportunity.

A shifting market can force many tough and difficult decisions in your commercial brokerage business. Make no mistake: You simply can't afford to bury your head in the sand or pretend the glory days of the boom market will return. You will have to make adjustments to your personal and business expenses and possibly your costs of sale, as well, to quickly return your business to a position of profitability and sustainability.

TACTIC #3
DO MORE WITH LESS – LEVERAGE

An entrepreneur is a guy who thinks outside of the box, a person who does not accept the conventional. He constantly asks "what if?", "could I?", or "should I?"

SAM ZELL, REAL ESTATE ENTREPRENEUR AND
CHAIRMAN OF EQUITY GROUP INVESTMENTS

In the opening pages of Dominic Dodd and Ken Favaro's compelling book *The Three Tensions*, a beleaguered manager asserts that he can either increase margins or volume but not both. What we love about this book is his coach's answer: He reminds the manager of a time when people lived in huts and were forced to make stark choices between heat and light. To have light, they needed to cut windows, which would allow the heat to escape. If staying warm was the goal, they faced the prospect of sitting in the dark. "The invention of glass made it possible to overcome this dilemma—to let in light, but not the cold. How then ... will you resolve your dilemma between no sales growth and no margin improvement? Where is the glass?"

As you reexamine your business in the wake of the shift, don't settle for conventional answers or solutions. Always be asking, "How can we break through and do this better, faster, cheaper? How can we do more with less?" Shifts can be creative catalysts and are legendary for creating new business models and driving innovation. Colgate, General Electric, Hershey, Dow Chemical, 3M, Disney, Texas Instruments, Mattel, and Microsoft highlight a long list of multibillion-dollar corporations born in recessions. *BusinessWeek*'s Reena Jana put it well in her July 2009 special report "Recession: The Mother of Innovation?" when she wrote: "Recessions can also help executives figure out how to improve products, services, and processes internally and for customers. Ideally, the creative thinking that's needed to weather the storm of an economic downturn can lead to new markets and revenue streams." In short, the same creativity you'll employ to discover ways to do more with less can easily lead you to earn more with less.

At first this may sound like a recipe for frustration. After all, conventional business wisdom holds that if you do more (scope), then you need to either bring more (not less) time or resources to the table or accept a drop in quality. The challenge in a shift is that you don't have any more time to give and your resources are strapped. And compromising on quality isn't an option—a broker's reputation, once tarnished, can take years to repair. The key to avoiding this catch-22: Invest your creative energy where it most matters—leverage your systems and your people.

THE SIX COMPETENCIES OF A SHIFTED BUSINESS

In good times, many brokers often battle more with more. As business ramps up, systems and people are amplified in lockstep. If, in the past, you required a certain amount of support to develop and close 10 deals, the tendency is to think you'll need three times as many resources to do 30 transactions. Even successful businesses can fall prey to this kind of faulty arithmetic. So as revenues rise, costs quietly creep up. Thankfully, what boom times conceal, shifts reveal. The *right* person can do what three *ineffective* people were trying to do. And the right person doesn't cost three times as much either! You can pay one person more than you paid the average of the other three and still come out way ahead financially. More efficient systems can dramatically increase productivity, as well.

One of the foundations of business growth is that a profitable business must consistently increase the efficiency of its assets to produce greater returns. The opportunity of a shift is to discover this because you don't have the luxury of not discovering it. In tough times, you wake up to the reality that you must work smarter. The only question is where to start? The answer is the six core competencies of a commercial real estate business (see figure 6).

THE SIX CORE COMPETENCIES OF A COMMERCIAL REAL ESTATE BUSINESS

1. Lead generate, capture, and convert appointments.

2. Present to prospects and get exclusive representation agreements.

3. Show properties to buyers/tenants and market properties for sellers/owners.

4. Write and negotiate contracts and lease agreements.

5. Coordinate the transaction from due diligence to close.

6. Manage your commissions.

Figure 6

These core competencies follow a precise order of priority, beginning with the most foundational. No matter your prowess at making presentations and winning client representation agreements, you can't deliver them without first generating and converting leads to appointments—the *foundation* of your success. Without exclusive representation agreements, you have no inventory to market or tenants to find properties for. After all the servicing is done and the transaction is closed, you have to manage your commission income and expenses so that you have a profit left at the end of the day. Each of the Six Core Competencies builds the foundation for the next, and altogether they represent your greatest priorities. A shift in the market invites you to take the wheel, since you no longer have the option of riding shotgun when it comes to the heart of your business: generating leads and converting them to representation agreements.

Just as you hold yourself accountable to putting first things first, focus your team on these priorities as well. The six core competencies can be your jeweler's loupe through which you examine your activities, systems, and people. Those who hew closest to the foundational competencies are revealed to be authentic gems: the rest need to be reeducated, refocused, or, if they are unable or unwilling to shine, released. This is what being "on top of your business" means: that everything and everyone is focused on the foundational competencies—the core activities that drive sustainability and profitability. You're reducing your business world back to what's important, and this will empower you to say no to all the other stuff. It gives you focus and energy, and puts you back in the position where you must always be doing what matters most. What you'll discover is that's what made you successful to begin with.

SYSTEMS LEVERAGE

Good markets make for sloppy systems—not because we don't care, but rather because we're so busy chasing deals. This is almost always a pay-me-now or pay-me-later situation, and we accept a certain level of chaos on the promise that the money we're earning today will finance fixing things tomorrow. However, as soon as the market starts to shift downward, that luxury is no longer appropriate or affordable. Now is the time to examine your systems to determine, first, if they are in alignment with your foundational competencies and, second, if they are being done well. As management guru Peter Drucker said, "There is nothing so useless as doing efficiently that which should not be done at all." In other words, strive first to be effective (to do the right things) and then to be efficient (to do things right).

In one of the top business bestsellers of all time, *The E-Myth Revisited*, Michael E. Gerber encouraged entrepreneurs to think of their business as a "franchise prototype." Why? Because franchises succeed 95 percent of the time, while more than 50 percent of independent businesses fail. Franchise-format businesses succeed because they rely on documented, proven, and repeatable systems for delivering everything from hamburgers to accounting services. It's no different for your commercial brokerage practice.

Your systems are the engines for driving business development, delivering customer service, as well as managing and maintaining your day-to-day business operations. They can be as humble as a checklist or a script, or as complex as your computer network. Some are written down, many are unwritten and internalized—but all should be documented. You may not even recognize what you do as a system, but your junior brokers or executive assistant could probably identify dozens of them. Every time you say something like, "Here, let me show you how to do that" or "Look, this is how we do it here," you're demonstrating your standards for how you expect your business to be run. Systems exist wherever you have standards, whether you are aware of them or not (see figure 7).

First, examine your lead generation and conversion systems. Are they being handled effectively? Is the right person supervising the process? In almost every case, the senior broker should be executing, directing, or at least directly supervising these systems. Besides the fact that no one will be more in tune with the market or better equipped to convert leads, no one takes more ownership of business development than the lead broker. When people own tasks, those tasks get done. Your executive assistant or junior broker may manage the database and execute drip or follow-up campaigns, but the messages, the offers, and the content are delivered through your experience and direct supervision.

As you assess your systems, trim the fat. If in the past you've purchased business directories or stacking plans, it's now time to shift. Do some prospecting, hire affordable workers to help you cold call and stack buildings, visit the local business library, and pay a few bucks to photocopy what you need! The shift spurred Mark Raccuia of Chicago to overhaul his presentation preparation system. He says, "Our team of four now does what we used to need six to eight people to do. The obvious benefit is expense cutting, but it has also added leverage to our work. This leverage comes from having an electronic platform that is uniform across the board. All of our portfolios and due diligence packages are standardized and any of us can push the button to send it out today." System leverage means getting to your customers faster, cheaper, and more efficiently. An

COMMERCIAL REAL ESTATE SYSTEMS

Lead Generation and Conversion Systems (Business Development)
1. Prospecting
     I.   Call Lists
     II.   Area / Building Stacking Plans
         • Identify Building Owners
         • Collect Rent Rolls and Tenant Profiles
         • Identify Decision Makers and Gatekeepers
     III. Networking Events
     IV.   Door-to-Door Canvassing
2. Marketing
     I.   Internet and Website Optimization
     II.   Signage
     III. Drip Campaigns (8 x 8, 33 Touch, 12 Direct)
     IV.   Brochures and Fliers

Administration and Support Systems (Processing)
1. Deliverables
     I.   Confidential Offering Memorandums and Pro Forma Financials
     II.   Research
         • Rental and Sales Comps
         • Market Analysis
         • Demographics
         • Traffic Studies
         • Property Condition Assessments
         • ADA Compliance
         • Environmental Site Assessments—Phases I, II, and III
         • Title, Zoning, and Building Code Reports
2. Closing Procedures
     I.   Transaction Management System
     II.   Title, Insurance, Escrow, and Mortgage
     III. Letter of Intent, Lease Agreements, and Purchase and Sale
           Documents
4. Database
     I.   CRM Software
     II.   Prospect Lists and Directory Acquisitions
     III. Maintenance (Inputting and Updating)
4. Back Office
     I.   Phone Systems
     II.   Office Supplies
     III. Vendor Agreements

Figure 7

old saying in commercial real estate is "time kills all deals," so in a shifted market it is even more important than ever to be able to respond quickly to all prospect inquiries.

With the right systems in place, your website can be one of your most efficient lead generation sources. While we will discuss websites in depth in "Tactic #6, Catch People in Your Web," a good first step is to ensure that you have a process in place that works the leads that come from your website in a timely manner. Today, Internet-empowered consumers expect instant gratification. Response times must be quick, with the best results coming from follow-up that happens within hours of receiving the lead. Every day that passes increases the likelihood that the potential client will move on to another more responsive broker. The issue is very few of us are chained to our desks, so systems here are vital. Autoresponders on your email can set expectations for later follow-up, calls can be forwarded to your cell, and your executive assistant or junior broker can be taught simple scripts for immediate response and follow-up. Ben Kinney, a top broker in Bellingham, Washington, has engineered his systems so efficiently that his team often reaches out to potential clients while they are still on his site!

In a shift, transactions can be fewer and farther between, and if you don't have the right system in place to manage them, you'll potentially miss out on opportunities. An online transaction management system can be a wise investment of your resources. "I worked for years without this type of system," said Steven McMurtrie, executive director of commercial real estate offices in Michigan and California. "Realistically, today, you can't work without it. In this market, you have to put a lot in the pipeline, and you can't manage all of those transactions effectively without this type of system."

A good transaction management system allows for easy access to all information about a transaction by all parties, in a secure and confidential way. It eases the process of review and approvals, and it communicates the progress of the transaction as key milestones are met. It captures all details in one location and helps you ensure that nothing is overlooked. Steven adds, "We can't afford to lose any transactions in this market due to oversights."

As a senior broker, you have to use systems to leverage talent. If you are spending excess time managing your team, you aren't focused on business development, your most crucial role. Steven has seen the transformation in his management practices and his team firsthand.

At the end of the day, you want to be able to "turn off" your business for a while and focus on your family and friends. Without an effective contact management system, you will never be able to leave your "business" behind. You will always be haunted by the nagging thought that you forgot to call someone, or send information they needed. A good contact management system will manage these details and allow you to clear your mind and give your family and friends the attention they deserve.

David Neault,
Norco, California

"The system offers project management, but also broker management and collaboration management. My job is to review transactions on a weekly basis and make sure that every transaction is moving forward. I've gone in and salvaged projects because there's no lag—it doesn't take days to uncover a problem. We want brokers to be successful. With this type of project management, we can catch issues before they become real problems."

Regardless of the systems you have in place, first devote your attention to the processes and systems that are in the direct path of revenue. In a shifting market, 100 percent of your team—even executive assistants and research staff—must have lead generation as a priority. Then, cast your eye on the back-office systems that can be done more quickly or cheaply. In some cases, you may discover processes that are simply being done for their own sake or to make life just a little easier—these are the first to go.

PEOPLE LEVERAGE

If you've been in the commercial real estate industry for some time, you're familiar with the old-school career growth path. You aspire to the ideal of a partnership where you share a pool of business. You start out in a junior position, partnering with other experienced brokers on a small percentage of business, and keep working your own deals. As you gain experience, you move into the senior position and begin hiring junior brokers, bringing more on as fast as business will allow. They're supposed to do the legwork while you use your talents to convert and close. You hope they earn their keep, but they're green and you have to invest time and money toward training them. All the while, you're still working hard to develop and close deals. Over time, you bring on teams of junior and senior brokers—you get the house split of their business, but your overhead grows and you are spending more and more time managing rather than making the best use of your experience and talents. No matter what, you're always working hard in the business to achieve the success you want, but because your income is increasingly diluted, you have to gross more and more to net the same amount.

The problem with the old-school approach is that it assumes the pool is big enough to share and that you have the time and resources to oversee a larger and larger team. In a shifted market—when that pool shrinks or even becomes a vortex, pulling you under when your time is increasingly precious—you have no choice but to abandon that old-school ship. In a shift, the new school is your life raft.

The new school is all about leverage: Leveraging your talents and knowledge and the productivity of the people who work with you to produce the maximum income (see figure 8 on p. 40). In a shifted market, the broker who has the most leads to chase and the most transactions in the pipeline wins, so using people wisely and cost-effectively to generate leads and get deals done is the only survival technique that matters. The new school recognizes the leverage to be found in the paid prospector, the executive assistant, and the commercial operations manager. More than that, it presents a path—in good times or bad—to a different kind of future for you: one in which you are a business owner managing one or more profitable organizations, rather than somebody who is constantly working within the pool for his fair share. The new school offers you the flexibility to continue to operate in your business in a more limited way or to work on your businesses as a high-level leader.

When you're tired of doing it all, it's prime time to find a paid prospector (see step 2 of figure 8). When I first relocated my commercial practice to San Diego, I had to build my business from the ground up and knew that I had to be efficient with my time and money. I hired college students to stack buildings and, when they had learned their scripts, cold call to identify gatekeepers and decision makers. The best of these paid prospectors earned the right to call lower-tier prospects and set appointments for presentations. I handled the larger prospects and the presentations were my unique domain.

New-School Commercial Brokerage Career Path

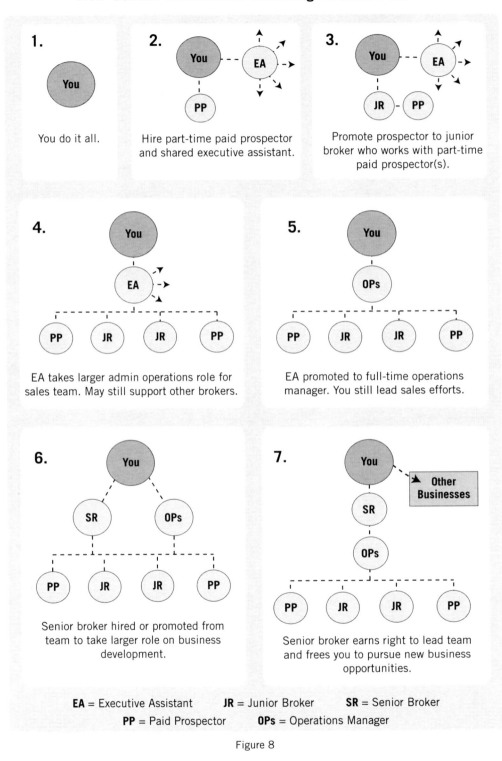

1.

You do it all.

2.

Hire part-time paid prospector and shared executive assistant.

3.

Promote prospector to junior broker who works with part-time paid prospector(s).

4.

EA takes larger admin operations role for sales team. May still support other brokers.

5.

EA promoted to full-time operations manager. You still lead sales efforts.

6.

Senior broker hired or promoted from team to take larger role on business development.

7.

Senior broker earns right to lead team and frees you to pursue new business opportunities.

EA = Executive Assistant   **JR** = Junior Broker   **SR** = Senior Broker

PP = Paid Prospector   **OPs** = Operations Manager

Figure 8

Paid prospectors are powerful tools, yet maybe only 10 percent of brokers use them. They can be incredibly cost-effective, and in a down economy, it's not hard to find driven people hungry to prove themselves. You can pay them a modest hourly wage or per lead generated. The leverage power behind paid prospectors is flexibility: You pay them to do what you need them to do, and sometimes only if they produce. Ben Kinney hires people to cold call, offers them $40 per appointment booked, and doesn't pay them until they book ten. If they can't generate ten every two weeks, it's time to part ways. Once prospectors prove their drive and talents—that they are true athletes—you can train them to do more. They may grow into junior brokers who share your passion for commercial real estate and who have shown a knack for business development (step 3 of figure 8). Have them focus on lower-tier prospects, where the risk is lower if they drop the ball.

An added benefit of paid prospectors is the energy they bring. In a time when the doldrums can kill a brokerage, paid prospectors can revive the drive and spirit of competition in everybody around them. Success begets success. When junior brokers and even senior brokers see the prospectors hitting the streets and generating leads, they're inspired to step up their own game.

While leveraging your team for lead generation is a critical first step, you need to ensure you have the support in place for handling those leads. If you hire wisely, an executive assistant can be the operational athlete you need to double your income (see steps 2 and 3 of figure 8). In the best of times, they clear your plate of mundane processing tasks, freeing you up to convert and close. In the worst of times, they should have the drive and bandwidth to take on any task you throw at them—and that task should be lead generation. You may have thought of executive assistants as processors of transactions—handling marketing presentations, surveys, and the like—but exceptional EAs are organizational dynamos, and they should be able to feed your database, generate prospect lists, manage drip campaigns, and even follow up with leads from your website. All it takes is a bit of training and some scripts.

That said, training and scripts won't help if you haven't hired the right talent. Most brokers hire assistants for assistance; few hire for the ability to bring leadership to the tasks at hand. They are quick to hire, assuming that administrative tasks don't require much skill. They're looking for a body to put in a seat; instead, they should be slow to hire and quick to fire. Top teams recruit and select talent—at every level. They identify the specific needs of the position, they explore how to identify top-tier recruits, they conduct behavioral assessments, and they invest the necessary time in training. When hiring for support, don't focus on an executive assistant—look for an assistant executive.

The tough reality of a shifted market is that you may have even less support than you once had. The executive assistant you used to share with two or three brokers, you may now share with five or six. That's the right way to start. You don't need the full salary of an assistant until you know they can pull their weight and truly help you grow your business. During the shared assistant phase, you may think that your assistant just doesn't have the time to do more for you. That's rarely the case, though. You just have to decide what you are willing to keep on your plate (possibly some processing tasks) and how you can use the time you have with the assistant most effectively. And you never know what a person can handle until you push him/her. In a shifted market, everybody on your team should recognize that they will have to work harder to keep their income.

If your executive assistant is talent and your team grows, it may be time to bring that individual on full time (see step 5 in figure 8). The full-time EA can handle all the systems and administrative work for your large team, just like they handled the needs of several senior brokers in the past. They will also enjoy a more stable, predictable workday, which is a nice bonus for all.

An executive assistant can also be elevated to a commercial operations manager if the talent is there (see step 6 in figure 8). "We had to have a commercial operations manager to manage the program and assist the brokers," explained Steven McMurtrie when describing their transaction management system. The commercial operations manager provides support to all of the brokers by managing the system, handling the preliminary listing paperwork, inputting it into the system, etc. And he/she does it for brokers across multiple offices. Steven is able to leverage that person's talents with minimal cost to support brokers and keep them in the field doing business development work—leverage that is only possible because they have a centralized, online system. "In markets without a commercial operations manager, we've lost members, particularly junior brokers, because they don't have enough support. And for junior brokers, that support is essential."

In the new school, there is still plenty of room for junior brokers, but the key is to build up your pool of income before you let other people share it. If you are using paid prospectors to improve your income stream, the junior brokers have to prove their worth by being more valuable (generating more *net* income) than the paid prospectors. It may be time to see if they can step up and earn their keep. In a shifted market, in particular, you can't feed junior brokers forever. If they can convert and close, bring on their own clients, start generating referral business, they've proven their worth to the business.

And if you're a junior broker, be on notice. When there's not enough business to go around, the number of commercial real estate agents can plummet. The question you have to ask yourself is whether you have the drive to stay in it. And if you do, you need to start proving yourself now!

More than likely, most broker teams will shift with the market. When the pool shrinks, you might pare your team back to one junior broker and hire a paid prospector. Or you might shift your executive assistant to doing more of the work that a paid prospector might do, if the drive and skill set are there. Regardless of who you have on your team, in a shifted market, it is essential that every member have a responsibility for new business development.

Ultimately, you have to ask yourself: Are the people working for me providing a real return on the investment I'm making in them? In a shifted market, you want true, outsized talent—the athletes—on your team. A shift is a perfect time to pick them up, but only if it's talent that can produce for you. And while good talent may be more available, talent wants to grow, so even in a down market, you need a value proposition to attract the best.

When the market comes back around, you may be able to hire "nice to have" leverage again—specialists, support roles, and the like. But even in a good market, the answer to the question, "Will my net income go up?" better be a resounding yes. Only then can you feel confident that the person will earn his/her keep by generating cash flow and will help you create cash reserves that you can leverage when the market shifts again.

The gift of the shift for commercial brokers is that you have the opportunity to invest in the people and processes that create the most leverage and better utilize your time and talents. Base your investments on sound financial principles: Where will you get the greatest return? And remember the basic rule of the Pareto Principle—20 percent of your efforts produce 80 percent of your results. For every person, process, and task you perform, ask yourself, "Is this a 20-percenter or an 80-percenter?" Do your best to get rid of the 80 percent of time- and money-wasters and leverage the rest.

TACTIC #4
FIND THE MOTIVATED –
LEAD GENERATION

The difference between involvement and commitment is like ham and eggs. The chicken is involved; the pig is committed.

MARTINA NAVRATILOVA,

NINE-TIME WIMBLEDON SINGLES CHAMPION AND

WINNER OF FIFTY-NINE GRAND-SLAM TITLES

It's hard to motivate a real estate team when pipelines are drying up. Chris Sands, of Los Angeles, California, was struggling to do just that, so he called his team together for a little education on the basics: "When you're driving to an appointment, or to the office, or to your home in the evening, the best thing you can do is use that time wisely. Look for properties that need representation and ask, 'Is it in our database?' Always be on the lookout for a property owner who needs our help." A few days later, a junior broker noticed an old department store that was vacant and boarded up. He found that the property had been purchased by a multi-family development group at the top of the market for about $43 million with $30 million financed by a local bank. But as the market shifted, they couldn't develop the property. With their debt burden and the lower market valuations, they were upside down and had stopped making payments.

Chris and his team contacted the bank and discovered that they were willing to consider a short sale. The team marketed the property and quickly found an interested big-box retailer that would pay $17.5 million for it, which the bank was actually willing to accept. But meanwhile, the property owner had found a new investor. The influx of funds coupled with the bank's willingness to lower the note amount allowed them to hold onto the property and revise their plan to develop it. The property owners were happy because they were able to validate the property valuation and renegotiate the loan; the bank was happy because the loan was performing again. Even though Chris did not close the transaction, he did close two subsequent transactions with the big-box retailer as a result of presenting this off-market opportunity, and he strengthened his relationship with the bank as well as developed a strong relationship with the existing property owners, opening up new listing opportunities.

"We create relationships and we are problem solvers. That's what we do," explained Chris. "When you look for problems to solve and people to meet, you will find the motivated."

Know your prospective clients; know your market. This is a mantra of smart business management. And in a shifted market, commercial real estate brokers must put this mantra into practice. If you wait for the media to tell you what potential clients may need or want, you'll be months behind the competitive curve. To stay ahead of it, your only option is to go directly to the source—and that means prospecting.

Prospecting offers two benefits in a shifted market: leads and knowledge. Both are crucial to your survival.

When times are lean, lead generation takes more skill and more grit. It takes *MASSIVE ACTION*—cold calling, canvassing, referral networking, web-based marketing, and more. With fewer motivated investors, poor credit conditions, and valuations that lag due to market conditions, the competition for viable leads is fierce. And you will likely have to put twice as many leads into the production pipeline during a shifted market to earn the same income, given the higher rate of deal fallout and general investor and tenant malaise. To survive, you have to do whatever it takes. As Gary Keller puts it, "In a shift you may have to concede that the real estate pie is smaller. Okay. Now go get your *unfair share*."

The bonus of the hard work of prospecting is developing an intimate understanding of your market. It's a highly effective form of lead generation, and it also builds market expertise. While market shifts may have similar attributes on a macro level—lax loan standards, overbuilding, economic recession—on a micro level, every shift is different and every market is unique. Only by understanding the nuances of your current market can you target your business development activities to generate the best leads and the greatest return on your time, money, and effort. If you aren't prospecting—actually talking with people in your market—how can you discover their current pain and the current market trends? How can you discover the most relevant motivators? If you wait to learn about these motivators from the media or other real estate professionals, you'll be dead in the water.

Each broker in every national shift experiences his own regional and local shift as well. Savvy real estate professionals must evaluate how their local shift is linked to the regional and national shift, and make adjustments to stay ahead of the curve. They must react to the "shift" by hitting the basics hard, working with past contacts, cold calling, and by seeking creative ways to leverage the fact that they are among the best and most experienced brokers in their market when it comes to helping their clients. They must use their contacts to list properties for sale or lease, and then develop creative ways to find buyers or tenants.

In short, they must find ways to leverage their experience and contacts to diversify their practice and gain market share or they will simply drop out.

Mark Hughes,
San Diego, California

Prospecting helps you develop the messaging you need for targeted, effective marketing. This is the essence of the prospecting-based, marketing-enhanced approach that will keep revenue flowing in a shift.

PROSPECTING BASED, MARKETING ENHANCED

In a shifted market, you need to be more efficient, more targeted, and more cost-effective. You can't waste money on costly business development practices—or any other practices—that aren't generating a net return on investment. Recall the lessons in cost cutting from Tactic #2. Prior to a shift, you might be flush enough to spend revenue on advertising or other activities that generated brand awareness and a few viable leads, but in a shifted market, every dollar and every hour counts. If it isn't getting you closer to an appointment, you need to stop doing it.

But in a shifted market, you also can't cut your business development efforts in half—*you need to double them*. So prospecting activities must take priority over most marketing activities, which are often too costly and too limited on returns. Besides, to make your marketing work, you need to understand how to target your messaging and you need listings to market—two needs you can fulfill through prospecting. Tactic #6 offers powerful revelations about web-based marketing, which should be the starting point for all of your marketing efforts. Figure 9 shows business development activities ranked for a shifted market in terms of cost-effectiveness and lead generation efficiency.

In a prospecting-based, marketing-enhanced business development model, the goal is to find the motivated by doing less of what doesn't work and more of what does. You need to answer the questions, "What forms

BUSINESS DEVELOPMENT IN A SHIFTED MARKET

PROSPECTING

1. **Cold Calling**: Like Nike says, "Just do it!"

2. **Referral Prospecting**: A shifted market is a prime opportunity to ask clients for referrals.

3. **Cold Canvassing**: Know your market better than your competitors.

4. **Broker-to-Broker Referrals**: Go beyond friends and clients—develop relationships with residential agents and other commercial brokers.

5. **Networking**: Target, target, target your networking efforts to those that actually generate leads, not merely build brand awareness.

MARKETING

1. **Online and Social Marketing**: It's a new world; embrace it. We'll show you how in Tactic #6.

2. **Signs**: Turn sign leads into new buyer and tenant clients. Secure commercial listings that have high visibility signage opportunities. If a prospect is not interested in your listing from a sign call, secure a meeting so you can help them find more viable properties.

3. **Media Presence**: Use articles, interviews, and other media appearances to prove your expertise and garner name recognition. Reach out to the media to make sure you're the one they call when they need an interview. This is free advertising for you and your commercial practice.

4. **Advertising**: Only advertise wins—closed transactions perhaps—and then only with priority, high-profile clients, so the the advertising benefits you both.

5. **Mailings**: "If you mail, you fail" may not be true 100 percent of the time, but it's true most of the time, so use print mailings and emailings only as part of a broader strategy.

Figure 9

of lead generation are working for me?" "What messages and offers are resulting in appointments, clients, and closed deals?" "What are my strongest, most profitable income streams?" Then target your business development efforts accordingly. In the following sections, we'll highlight what we believe are the most effective lead generation strategies for a shifted market.

COLD CALLING

Do NOT skip this section of the book. And don't say that you don't like to cold call—no one does! Yes, you will face rejection with perhaps as much as 95 percent of cold-call prospects. But ask yourself this question: "Is your *desire to succeed stronger* than your aversion to cold calling?" If so, then you will just do it—every day. Why? Because no other prospecting technique is as effective in helping you reach new prospects and uncover the hidden opportunities in the market. In most cases, baseball players who hit the most home runs also tend to lead the league in strikeouts; but like the great Babe Ruth said, "Never let the fear of striking out get in your way."

Cold calling is not a new tactic, but because nobody really likes to do it, we all let it slide the moment we have a decent pipeline. Only a handful of top brokers avoid this trap, which, by the way, is exactly why they are top brokers. Because we stop doing it, we get rusty. In a shift, you must have a structured, accountable cold-calling program that leverages the depth of your contact database, the skills of every person on your team, and the power of a targeted approach.

A measure of your lead-generating success is the number of valid contacts in your customer relationship management (CRM) database, which should identify cold, warm, and hot prospects to ensure that you spend your time wisely. A general rule of thumb is that your database should include at least 2,000 cold prospects, 250 warm prospects, and 50 hot prospects at any given time. Many brokers struggle during a shifted market simply because their database of prospects is too small. If your current market area cannot support this many prospects, then you need to consider expanding your geographic boundaries. Or

Business development is a constant focus for our commercial team of brokers, and getting accurate information on prospects and owners of commercial properties is task number one. By utilizing our great relationship with Stewart Title to help in these efforts, we save enormous time and resources that we can focus directly on our prospecting efforts.

Darrow Fiedler,
Boise, Idaho

you may need to expand your brokerage skill set, such as including retail or industrial prospects if your previous brokerage background was primarily office space. We'll talk more about expanding your expertise to pursue markets of the moment in Tactic #11.

With a strong database, you can leverage your team effectively. Your assistant generates call lists, paid prospectors handle most of the cold leads, junior brokers handle warm prospects, and you, as senior broker, handle hot prospects. That said, in a shift, you may not have enough hot leads to keep you busy. The moment that happens, you should be working on warm and cold ones or finding ways to add hot leads to your database. Nobody on the team should be rusty when it comes to tackling cold calls, including you.

More importantly, every member of your team should be one component of an overall targeted approach. Target geographical areas, certain industries, companies facing certain problems or presenting certain opportunities, as well as ideal buyers or tenants for your properties. "It's easier to make one hundred calls if they are all to learn the same thing," explains Mark Raccuia of Chicago. "Having focus and targets is essential to leveraging my energy."

In Charlie Lockwood's brokerage in Atlanta, they take a consultative approach to cold calling. "We think about the potential client, look at the problems the prospect is having, and build our conversations around those issues rather than pitching our solution," he explained. "You become a potential problem solver rather than a salesperson. Does a tenant need to downsize? Does a landowner need to sell to become more liquid? Does a buyer need an acquisition to complete a 1031 exchange? *Problem-focused cold calling* makes opening conversations effortless. This is the most powerful shift you can make." If you take this approach and target prospects with specific problems (such as excess office space after downsizing, a property that's been on the market for more than a year, etc.), the calls will be smooth and effective, naturally showcasing your expertise.

As a commercial broker, you have tremendous access to demand data. This gives you the advantage. With STDBonline (Site To Do Business) and other sources, you can marry demand to supply and generate quality leads. Mac McClure saw that a client in Orlando owned a building that was half full. "We discovered that there were no paint stores in a several mile radius. We then went to the big paint stores and got them bidding for the opportunity to move into the building. Now I have a client because of my access to data and my willingness to help." Proactive lead generation is finding industries or pockets of potential clients and learning enough about them that you can bring them information about how they can keep their business or expand it. "If I can help the owner of a business," says Mac, "I have a client for life."

As you execute your system, you must remember that the fundamental purpose of any cold call is to convince the prospect that meeting with you for thirty minutes is worth his or her time. While a little probing for pain is necessary to help you identify problems you can help solve, you aren't trying to solve the problems over the phone. Commercial real estate is a "press the flesh" business—meeting face-to-face with new prospects is the best way to grow your client base. In Tactic #5, scripts are offered to help you get those meetings.

Maintain constant contact with the people you have done business with because they always have needs until they die or retire.

Charles "Mac" McClure,
Dallas, Texas

A derivative of cold calling is what's often referred to as "warm calling," and in a shift, one goal of warm calling is proactive cultivation. There are prospects and clients in your database who don't currently need your services, and you know that. But if they never hear from you, when they do need your services, are you the person they'll call? In commercial real estate, the ultimate goal is to create a lifelong client, and the only way to do that is to develop a personal and professional relationship. So call to talk to them about their personal interests, their family, and so on. Offer to take them to lunch or to play golf; invite them to events you think they might enjoy. "I call and ask about their lives and ask how I can help, like a friend would," says Mark Bratton of Honolulu, Hawaii. "I am genuinely interested. If I hear that they're selling tickets to a charity event, I am interested. If they're recruiting volunteers for a beach clean-up, I'm on the list. This is about connecting with others for no particular reason, no specific expected gains."

Also use the opportunity to discover what is currently important to them, how business is going, *what problems they face*. Offer information about the state of the market and the types of commercial real estate they might be interested in. The goal of this relationship building is to insulate your relationship with your client. Other brokers will be calling them *all the time*, so make sure they receive calls from you on a regular basis.

Regardless of whether it's the first or the fortieth time you've talked to a client, to get their attention, be focused on *their* problems.

REFERRAL PROSPECTING

Commercial real estate is a referral-based business, so you should know how to ask for a referral from a happy client. But in a shifted market, you need to do more than ask; you need to make referrals happen through massive action!

When I had closed a deal for a client, I would schedule a meeting where I would ask for their feedback on my performance and the overall result. At the end of that discussion, I wouldn't just ask for referrals—I would make it happen: "Mr. Client, I'm sure you know people who might need my services now or in the future," I would begin. "I'd like you to open your database and give me the names of four or five people I can use your name with." And I wouldn't leave the office until I had those names. You'd be surprised how many people are receptive to a direct approach. In fact, businesspeople tend to be more than receptive—they respect it.

You actually have an advantage in a shifted market: Your clients are likely facing tough financial situations. What is the second-largest line item expense on most companies' income statement? Real estate costs or rent. If you can substantially impact that line item, you are their savior. This is the ultimate opportunity to ask for a referral; they are grateful, willing to help. You just need to give them an opportunity to do so.

COLD CANVASSING

Cold canvassing is really just cold calling in person. So for most brokers, it has equal appeal—meaning none at all. But there is no better way to learn a market intimately than to walk a 3-to-5-mile area in the middle of the day, meeting tenants, exploring the buildings, talking with owners. Differentiating yourself through detailed knowledge of a market is a powerful competitive edge in a shift, one that we'll explore more in Tactic #5.

A young man—who was just getting started as a commercial broker and was trying to make his way through a challenging market—asked Reagan Dixon, from Dallas, Texas, for advice. Reagan, who is one of the top commercial real estate coaches in North America with more than forty years of experience, told him about one of the best ways to make money quickly: specialize in one area, a very small area. "For example," he suggested, "look at this one particular corner in Dallas, Texas: there are three office buildings located on that corner. Canvass to learn everything you can about those three buildings, their tenants, what kinds of deals the landlords are making. Once you get to know the tenants, ask to meet with them when you know their leases are up for renewal, and offer to get them the best deal in any one of those three buildings. You'll be able to do this because no one else is going to be as much of an expert on those three buildings on that one corner as you will be." The young broker did exactly as Reagan advised, becoming a tenant rep specializing in the buildings on that exact corner—and he made money quickly in a tough market.

What Reagan revealed to the young man is the heart of our argument: If you want to make money in a shifted market, you have to develop deep market knowledge and expertise, and you may have to specialize to make it happen fast. But regardless of your specialty, canvassing is going to be crucial to the development of that expertise.

You have opportunities every day to canvass—as you drive home, as you shop, as you go to dinner. When you are running errands, advises Gary Keller, "Strike up a conversation with store owners, and drive the conversation to the amazing tenant's market in the leasing segment. 'If I could get you a better location, cheaper rent, and possibly even have your new landlord buy out your current lease, would you be interested in meeting to discuss this further?'" Cold canvassing provides opportunities for brokers to master market knowledge and to make direct, powerful proposals to potential clients. Few lead generation tactics allow you to build rapport as quickly or to showcase your value proposition so starkly.

Recall the story from Chris Sands at the beginning of the chapter, and recognize that to really develop a keen eye for opportunities, you should look for problems to solve.

BROKER-TO-BROKER REFERRALS

In a shift, resistance is at an all-time high, and referrals are the surest path around that resistance. The time you spend building your referral network is invaluable. While you may be able to leverage referrals from clients, friends, and family, you'll be in harsh competition with other brokers for referrals from people in your community's business network. You need to find a source of referrals that is being disregarded by other brokers. That source? Residential real estate agents.

Our research has shown that residential real estate agents are the number one resource for referral networks. They know local communities, they know people, and they develop personal relationships with their clients, discovering information about their businesses, their property investments, and more. Yet these agents typically do *not* know commercial real estate, nor do they want to. Consequently, residential agents are almost totally disregarded as a referral source by commercial agents. Yet they, like you, are looking for opportunities to monetize their relationships and would jump at the chance to earn referral fees. If you launch yourself into this network and educate agents on the benefits of referrals, you'll be accessing an untapped resource that could make you a market leader.

To tap this resource, you have to expand your network to include residential agents, spend some time educating them, and let them know about successful referrals.

STEPS TO DEVELOPING REFERRAL RELATIONSHIPS WITH RESIDENTIAL AGENTS

1. Build your network.
2. Educate agents through one-on-one or group meetings.
3. Keep the referring agent in the loop.
4. Publicize successful referrals.

Figure 10

You may work in a brokerage that has both commercial and residential teams. If so, that's your starting point for developing your network. Those agents may be a bit more informed about commercial real estate or be more incentivized to pass referrals to brokers in the same company. But you shouldn't stop there. In any city there are vast numbers of real estate companies and agents for you to approach, vast opportunities for *massive action*.

Call the head of one of these companies, ask if you can come to the office and meet with the agents to educate them on the opportunities to earn income through commercial referrals. Propose a mutually beneficial relationship. A note of caution: If you expect them to send referrals your way, you had better be prepared to do the same for them. If you're in the midst of a shift, it's likely that they are too, and so they are just as motivated to build their referral networks.

As you educate agents, focus on the following:

- The complexities and liabilities inherent in commercial real estate brokerage
- The economics of referral fees – Simply showing your network the math involved with high-stakes commercial brokerage referral fees can motivate them to keep their eyes and ears open for opportunities to pass along to you.
- The key buzzwords to listen for and scripts to get referrals – Give them specific phrases or concepts that indicate a potential opportunity. You want them to send you viable leads and to prequalify them to some degree.
- The referral system – You must develop an easy-to-follow referral system they can use to gather and communicate information about

prospects. Develop a referral form like the one in figure 11, educate agents on each part of it, leave copies with them, and put it on your website.

SAMPLE REFERRAL FORM

DATE _____

Referred Person _____ Phone _____ Email _____
Referring Agent _____ Phone _____ Email _____
Receiving Agent _____ Phone _____ Email _____

TYPE OF TRANSACTION
____Buyer ___Seller ___Tenant ___Landlord ___1031 Exchange

TYPE OF PROPERTY
___Retail ___Office ___Industrial (Warehouse/Manufacturing)
___ Hospitality (Hotel) ___Business Service (Office and Storage)
___Multifamily ___Land ___Business

CONTACT RELATIONSHIP
____Client ___Family ___Friend ___Acquaintance ___Just-Met
- Have you worked on a transaction with this person?
- What was the outcome of the transaction?
- What is the person's behavioral style (DISC)?

CONTACT INFORMATION
- Who is the decision maker?
- Has the person completed a similar transaction before?
- What is his/her motivation?
- How soon does he/she need to act?
- What are his/her financial resources?
- Has he/she been working with other agents?
- Will he/she sign an exclusive agreement?
- Other important information:

Figure 11

- The importance of follow-up – To make sure referrals are not just a shot in the dark, the referral source needs to follow up with the prospect and motivate him to engage with you.

- Commercial market developments – Educate the residential agents on what is happening in the commercial market, particularly in your areas of expertise or the geographic areas in which you specialize. Discuss new retail or office developments, new road systems, new businesses moving into the marketplace, and so on. This will provide your residential agents a competitive advantage against their own residential competition.

This market education and training can be done in ten to twenty minutes and can be the basis for building a long-term relationship with these agents. Along with the referral form, leave behind any scripts you've developed that can help them identify and qualify leads for you.

"If you go into a residential office and you ask the question, 'How many of you have given a commercial referral?' you'll see many hands raised," said Steven McMurtrie, executive director of real estate offices in northern California. "If you then ask, 'How many of you got paid for a referral or know what became of it?' 100 percent of the time you'll get fewer hands." When you receive a referral, it is essential to keep the referring agent in the loop throughout the process. You may need to ask for them to use any influence they have with the prospect to help you convert that individual to a client. But also, it's good business. We mentioned transaction management systems in the previous tactic, and they can be used to both track a referral and keep the referring person appraised of its status, which will help your referral program be more successful. With

Steven's transaction management system, residential agents have access to enter referrals and then track them. However you do it, make sure you don't leave a referring agent out in the cold.

Nothing sells like success. For every referral that leads to a closed deal or a new client, be sure to thank your referral source, send them the referral fee that was promised, and then publicize the successful referral to other residential agents. When you consistently communicate the referral fees you pay—through emails, in newsletters, at networking events—you'll motivate your network and remind them of the benefits.

Charlie Lockwood tells a great story about a residential agent who became aware of a vacant commercial lot in Atlanta that was being foreclosed on. She was meeting with the banker about residential properties, so before her meeting, she contacted the commercial team in her office and brought them in on the deal. They soon developed a strong partnership between the residential agents and the commercial brokers to handle much of the bank's varied real estate needs.

> *The problem with referrals is that they can take you anywhere and everywhere. You might get inundated with referrals that are outside of your area of specialization. We used to say, "Give that referral to me." Now we say, "Give those referrals to US." We share referrals, and the more that I give out, the more that seem to come in. If a referral comes in that is outside of what you do, pass it on to a specialist in that field.*
>
> *Scott Miller,*
> *Minneapolis, Minnesota*

While residential agents are the most untapped resource, don't be afraid to seek out other commercial brokers. I recommend expanding your areas of expertise in a shifted market, but you may only be able to take that so far. Working with brokers who specialize in other areas can help you both effectively leverage your skill sets, something we discuss more in Tactics #10 and #11. Develop a trusted network of brokers who specialize in areas other than yours or operate in other geographical areas, send leads their way, and ask them to send relevant leads back to you.

Cold calling, referral prospecting, cold canvassing, and broker-to-broker referrals are proven lead generation tactics in a shift. They cost little but require more of your time and effort. There's no avoiding that reality, so you may as well not fight it. Networking, which shouldn't require a long explanation here, is another clear, proven way to get face-to-face with potential clients and referral partners. So get out your calendar and make a commitment to getting back in the mix. Lastly, the only marketing technique from figure 9 we'll cover in depth is online and social marketing, covered at length in Tactic #6. The rest, like networking, are more or less self-explanatory.

TO FIND THE MOTIVATED, YOU HAVE TO BE THE MOTIVATED

Early in my career, I recognized a critical truth that I think has been key to my success: I needed a way to hold myself accountable daily and weekly for business development. If I didn't have accountability, it would be too easy to let lead generation slide as my pipeline grew—and I'd seen what happened to brokers who stumbled down that path. So I gave my accountability partner a check for $1,000 made out to my biggest competitor in town. If I didn't meet my business development numbers in any given week, he would send the check to my competitor. Every week I felt the weight of that check as I cold called, canvassed, asked for referrals, and networked. If I missed my lead generation numbers, my partner wouldn't hesitate to put the check in the mail.

In a shifted market, it's not a $1,000 check hanging over your head; it's your *career*. If you're not disciplined in your business development efforts, if lead generation is not your top priority, if you aren't holding yourself and every person on your team accountable for this all-important goal, you risk a lot more than $1,000 … your very business could be forfeited to your competitors.

The problem most brokers face is that when the market is strong, you can get by on referrals, networking, and some light prospecting. You get a little busy, and serious lead generation falls off your schedule. You "know" that there will always be something in the pipeline … until one day there isn't. Suddenly you face a net income deficiency—because you've had a prospecting deficiency for some time. And now, when you need them the most, your prospecting skills may be rusty.

But a successful commercial broker in a shifted market has one overriding characteristic: commitment to doing the hard work that matters most in his business. That commitment is driven by accountability and discipline. Accountability certainly helped me maintain my focus on lead generation: My partner never had to send the check I gave him, and I hit my goals week after week. I couldn't afford not to. And you can't afford not to either.

As Gary Keller once said, "The most successful people are those who make regular appointments with themselves to do their most important work." It's incredibly easy to get distracted, to have your time consumed by needy clients and team members, to let discipline fall by the wayside. The solution? Time blocking—blocking out inviolable hours in your day that are devoted to business development and devoting most of your days to the deals most likely to close.

Which of the two schedules below looks most like yours?

COMMERCIAL HOBBY		COMMERCIAL CAREER	
10:00	Stroll into the office	7:30–9:00	Business development / prospecting / lead generation
10:00–11:00	Watercooler chat	9:00–11:00	Office work / emails / client calls
11:00–1:00	Lunch with fellow brokers	11:00–2:00	Meet with prospects and market canvassing
1:00–3:00	Call friends and clients with unsellable property	2:00–4:00	Office work / emails / client calls
3:30	Beat traffic and head home	4:00–5:30	Business Development Prospecting/Lead Generation

Figure 12

Most successful brokers choose to work on lead generation in the morning and late afternoon. The middle of the day is reserved for meetings and canvassing (traffic is much lighter, saving precious time). But you should establish a schedule you know will work for you.

To force himself to stop letting other appointments encroach on his prospecting time, Tony DiCello of Austin, Texas, former top broker and current director of MAPS Coaching, would take his paper calendar and color in blocks of time with black permanent marker so he couldn't write anything else in those time slots.

Hire a commercial coach or ask a mentor, partner, or even your spouse to hold you accountable for your business development efforts on a weekly basis. If you don't have some form of accountability, human nature will take over and your prospecting activities will suffer. Meet with your accountability partner once a week for five or ten minutes to go over your weekly activity. Hold them accountable as well. Have a penalty if either of you do not meet your weekly goals (dinner is on the "loser," for instance). By pushing and encouraging one another, you will both succeed.

You need to time block your week just as you time block your days—according to the requirements and opportunities of a shifted market. There will be far fewer home-run deals to be had, so you will need to focus your energy on the smaller deals—the singles and doubles—that are more likely to close and earn you revenue. The "hits" coming your way in a shifted market will get you from base to base, will keep your business afloat, so you need to spend the majority of your time on them. You might spend just one day a week practicing your big

If you can identify the most important thing you need to do every day to be a success and get that one thing done, you will be hugely successful. I do that every day. For me it is lead generation.

David Neault,
Temecula, California

swing—prospecting with potential home-run clients—to stay in shape for the deals that will eventually come your way again when the market improves.

Mark Bratton of Hawaii makes a practice of focusing on his bread-and-butter business activities four days a week. On those days, he spends a number of hours prospecting, making approximately forty cold or warm calls to find and follow up on leads. Mark reserves one day of the week for home-run practice. On this day, he focuses on a select list of billionaires and millionaires, regional mall owners, owners of fifty-story buildings, and captains of industry in his market. His intention is to be in communication with these people and to be of service. You can't lose all contact with your top-tier prospects and then hope they remember you when the market is on an upswing.

Regardless of exactly how you're blocking your time, you must not violate it. You may be afraid to say no to meeting requests, or you may just not want to, but sometimes you will have to do it. It's rare that team members, clients, or prospects don't have other openings in their schedules. Learn the word *no* and use it to keep you focused and disciplined in your business development efforts.

Walt Disney had a famous line about hard lessons: "You may not realize it when it happens, but a kick in the teeth may be the best thing in the world for you." Consider the shifted market a kick in the teeth that will motivate you to do what it takes to succeed. Take any and every opportunity to generate leads, to develop your business. In a shifted market, you have no choice. If you haven't prioritized prospecting and created a system based on discipline and accountability for you and your team, do it today. Don't let market doldrums invade your thinking and your business. Be targeted, be focused, be competitive, and go out and get your *unfair share*!

TACTIC #5
GET TO THE TABLE –
PROSPECT CONVERSION

My motto was always to keep swinging. Whether I was in a slump or feeling badly . . . the only thing to do was keep swinging.

HANK AARON, BASEBALL HALL OF FAMER

Today you are a different person than you were yesterday. At a cellular level, you've changed. Cells died off, new ones formed—all thanks to the miraculous process of cellular differentiation. Unique cells in your body wait on the sidelines for messages from your brain. In times of need, they are signaled to shift from a less specialized cell that plays a minimal role in the functioning of your body to a more specialized one that plays a critical role in keeping you alive. When you experience trauma, differentiation is part of your natural response. It's how you repair, grow, and survive.

Why the lesson on cellular biology? Because science offers powerful insights into how to deal with shifts in our environment. Our biological systems are focused on one thing: survival. And, in a shifted market, that's your focus too. To survive, you have to first recognize that your business is in a state of trauma: there are more unqualified prospects—time-wasters who don't have what it takes to get to a closed transaction—to wade through, and the few good prospects that remain are harder to convert than ever. In short, competition for signed exclusive agreements with qualified clients is brutal.

Your only option is to differentiate, to become more specialized in fulfilling the changing needs of prospects and clients in a shifted market. Think of Reagan Dixon's story of the young broker who became a specialist in one corner of real estate in Dallas. If you can't differentiate, your chances of survival are diminished.

Differentiation allows you to leverage your experience, market knowledge, specialized skill set, network, drive, creativity, and your accountability to establish yourself as a different breed of broker. It is the key to getting appointments with prospects so that you can accurately qualify them, and it's essential to converting the best prospects into clients, specifically clients who are likely to generate revenue through exclusive representation agreements. How effectively you leverage your talents, knowledge, and network to differentiate yourself throughout the conversion process will be the deciding factor in your ability to turn leads into appointments and prospects into quality clients—and possibly into net commission revenue.

Figure 13 depicts the aspects of differentiation you might rely on throughout the conversion process. From Tactic #4, you'll remember that during prospecting, the key is to be focused on problem solving with leads rather than selling your services. That focus continues as you try to convert those leads into appointments. Once you get an appointment, you leverage your specialized market knowledge and expertise to get a second meeting, where you differentiate your talents, services, and commitment through an accountable, creative, and proactive solution-based presentation to the client's problem.

The goal of your conversion efforts—which may be massive in a shifted market—is to get meetings that lead to exclusive agreements to

CONVERSION THROUGH DIFFERENTIATION

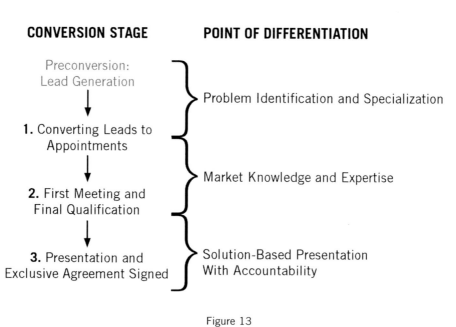

Figure 13

handle transactions that are likely to close. In a shifted market, I wouldn't suggest spending time on open listings unless you're absolutely convinced you have more or better information than your competition. You risk wasting time on deals that may never generate income when you could be working exclusive listings, which are more valuable even when they are smaller deals.

Remember, the best clients are looking for brokers with passion and drive. Differentiate yourself through your commitment to a closed transaction at every step of the process, and you'll find prospects and clients regularly choosing you over your competition.

1. DIFFERENTIATION TO CONVERT LEADS TO APPOINTMENTS

Converting leads to appointments is the most dollar-productive thing you can do every day. But you're not going to get the appointments you need unless you set yourself apart from the competition. What will make prospects pay attention is your ability to identify and show an understanding of their problems. Solving problems is the essence of what you do—you just need to highlight for the client how your skills and experience are a solid match for their particular problems. This unique ability is at the heart of your value proposition.

Remember, in a cold call or an initial contact, you aren't selling yourself, your company, or a particular commercial service—what you are "selling" is a *thirty-minute appointment*. Once you understand this truth, your conversion to appointments will go up dramatically. Most unsuccessful cold callers immediately launch into their five-minute pitch before they even understand the prospect's issues, which is why they are generally unproductive.

You must be prepared to do the following:

- Position yourself as a specialist.

- Qualify the prospect as a decision maker.

- Deal with two levels of objections.

- Find opportunities to get meetings.

Please understand that your most efficient results will typically come from direct communication on the phone and, occasionally, in person. Why? Because it's difficult to create a meaningful connection with their problem if you aren't having a conversation, even if you only have them on the phone for five minutes. Many attempt to avoid this reality check because they don't enjoy cold calling or prospecting. But it's the truth you must hear. Even with Internet lead generation and conversion (covered in Tactic #6), you'll just be leveraging technology to drive leads out of hiding. It's all about giving them value-add reasons to agree to meet with you. Think of it as a precursor to the core work of lead conversion.

Position yourself as a specialist. You may be a specialist in a geographic area, a property type, or a transaction type, but you have to *position* yourself as a specialist in solving the problems of the prospect. If the problem is paying too much rent or excess space, you're not just a commercial broker, you're a specialist in "tenant/owner negotiations and sublease dispositions"—a tenant representation specialist. If the problem is that a property isn't selling, you are not a generalist commercial broker, you are a specialist in "developing creative offers for nontraditional buyers"—a commercial investment specialist. And if you lack certain specialized knowledge or skills, leverage the expertise of your network throughout the conversion process.

It is better to get 50 percent of a successfully closed transaction than 100 percent of nothing. Specialize in solving shift-specific problems for clients and you will become known as the go-to expert; suddenly, prospects you were chasing will seek you out. You simply need to be the best in the marketplace at handling *their* business need.

> *If you continue to be a generalist, you will be simply chasing deals. When you become a specialist, the deals come to you.*
> *Darrow Fielder,*
> *Boise, Idaho*

Qualify the prospect as a decision maker. While qualifying leads is important, in a shifted market, prospects can be wary and uncertain. It's unlikely that you'll discover the truth of their situations until you meet with them face-to-face and establish rapport and trust. If you try to do too much qualifying on the phone, you may eliminate good leads based on limited or incorrect information. Commercial brokerage is a press-the-flesh business, so just focus on *getting meetings*. Once you're face-to-face, the qualification and rapport building can really begin.

Before asking for an appointment, the one thing you must do is determine if your prospect is the key decision maker. You need appointments with decision makers, not gatekeepers—don't waste time with people who can't get a transaction done. This author once spent two years working a transaction with a division president of a company, certain that he was the ultimate decision maker. However, I discovered that before the transaction could go through, the board of directors had to approve it. They didn't, and two years of work and a million-dollar commission was lost. Take it from me: Always make sure you fully understand the decision-making process for your client. Never assume—ask.

Deal with two levels of objections. The most important thing to remember when trying to get appointments with prospects is this: Probe—don't do the hard sell. For instance, your introduction should be very brief, with a broad value proposition based on your expertise and your company's services. For example:

- *Mr. Prospect, my name is Jane Smith and I am with [your brokerage]. We specialize in [your niche] in the [marketplace], and I'm calling to see if you are available next Tuesday for a brief thirty-minute business consultation to see how we can help you with your commercial properties.*

Now let's be realistic: Almost every person you call will object to your initial meeting request. It's just human nature—it's how we respond when we're inundated with proposals and opportunities. What I discovered in the more than 200,000 cold calls that I've made in my career is that getting past the objections is a two-phase process. My success rate was twice what other brokers who led with a five-minute value proposition were achieving, because I first deflected the generic "false" objection and *then* addressed the more "real" objection with a strong value proposition. And throughout, I continued to focus on the prospect's potential problem.

The first objection raised will almost always be generic, such as "I'm busy," "I'm not interested," "I'm working with someone else," "I don't have a need," or "I handle my real estate needs myself." *The most important first step is to deflect the objection by agreeing with it rather than try to argue with the prospect.* Sounds counterintuitive, but it works. Let's look at how to deflect some of the most common generic objections:

- **"I'm busy."** *Ms. Prospect, that's exactly why I'm calling you. In today's difficult economy, it is more important than ever for you to be focused on your core business. Our commercial services allow you to do just that. My firm can provide you with critical information and data that will help you make sound business decisions that are absolutely essential in today's difficult market. Are you available next Tuesday at ten o'clock for this business consultation, or does two o'clock work better for you?*

- **"I'm not interested."** *Mr. Prospect, I can appreciate the impersonal nature of this phone call, but I am totally convinced that when we meet, our firm will be of value and service to you and your company. I promise after we meet, if you do not see value in continuing our relationship, we will not call or contact you again unless you say so. Are you available next Tuesday at ten o'clock for this business consultation, or does two o'clock work better for you?*

- **"I'm working with someone else."** *Mr. Prospect, that is exactly why I am calling. Our firm has unparalleled market [coverage/knowledge/expertise] that I know can be of use and value to your firm . . . meaning more money in your firm's pocket at the end of the day. Are you available next Tuesday at ten o'clock for this business consultation, or does two o'clock work better for you?*

- **"I don't have a need."** *Ms. Prospect, that is exactly why I am calling. In today's ever-changing market, it is more important than ever to follow its pulse to allow you to make decisions quickly and efficiently. That's what our firm can provide to you . . . timely, accurate information and trends that allow you to make critical business decisions before the [market/rates] change. Are you available next Tuesday at ten o'clock for this business consultation, or does two o'clock work better for you?*

- **"I handle my real estate needs myself."** *Mr. Prospect, that is exactly why I am calling. In today's ever-changing market, it is critical to have independent, timely information to allow you to make sound business decisions. That's what our firm can provide to you . . . we are active in the market on a daily basis and our proprietary sources of information will allow you to make critical business decisions before the [market/rates] change. Are you available next Tuesday at ten o'clock for this business consultation, or does two o'clock work better?*

These deflecting scripts will help you probe for the real objection, where you begin to get some clarity about the prospect's problem. You may be able to close to a meeting after the first objection with these scripts, but that may not be the case. Instead, use the prospect's response to transition to a probing question about the real problems they face. When you discover the potential real objection to the meeting, which could be anything from "I'm locked into a lease for another two years" to "I feel like I need to give my current broker a few more months to get it sold," you can begin to truly differentiate yourself by better connecting your specific value proposition to their problem. Again, you are not trying to solve the problem over the phone, but you want to offer them possibilities of a solution and explain that if they meet with you, you'll be able to get to know them and their business, better assess the situation, and explore potential opportunities. Essentially, it's an opportunity for a free business analysis and diagnosis of their current situation, and that will make a thirty-minute meeting seem worth their time. Once you convince them of that, you can close to the appointment.

Conversion conversations require an individualized approach. Your prospects will detect an inauthentic script in a split second, so your scripts must be genuine and your own. You should leverage any information you already possess about the prospect and the problems faced, and you should adapt general scripts to focus on the most common problems present in your market. Leverage the information you've gathered through prospecting to adjust your scripts and highlight your expertise. If you are working with paid prospectors, they need to master baseline scripts, but you should then coach them in discovering their own rhythm and style.

These phone calls also present an opportunity to differentiate yourself through your passion. Buy a phone headset, stand up, and walk around your office while making your calls. Your prospect will feel the energy and passion in your voice and your success ratio of closing appointments will go up exponentially.

Find opportunities to get meetings. While phone or in-person conversations are the best way to get somebody to commit to meet with you, in a shifted market, you have to pursue all opportunities to convert leads to appointments. Following are some additional ideas to consider.

- If the prospect came as a referral, leverage the person that made the referral to help you. If you are not getting a response, ask the referrer to email or phone the prospect on your behalf.

- Mine the Internet for more information that can help you connect with the prospect. Find out who their clients are, who they partner with. Are any of these people or companies your clients? Use their LinkedIn profile to find connections you may share. Start your conversation with this information to help them see you as an existing connection, not a new, unknown entity.

- Mine your data sources to find new information about the local market that might pertain specifically to problems the prospect may face. Send the prospect an email and lead with this information. If you can share something they don't know, potential clients will perceive you as an expert, and that makes it easy to ask for and get an appointment.

- Make a direct, creative offer of free services to create a low-risk way for the prospect to agree to meet with you. Continue to differentiate yourself through problem identification and expertise. In our interviews, we found brokers were offering initial property valuations, consultations on space needs, or energy audits through partnerships with energy companies. Be careful, though, because in a shifted market, many unqualified prospects will want free information.

- Host educational events and invite current clients and key prospects (and possibly others in your network, such as residential real estate agents). You can differentiate yourself as an expert who understands the needs of the clients in the market, and prospective clients will mingle with existing ones and be able to hear their testimonials live.

Let it be said again: The most dollar-productive thing you can do with your time is to get appointments with potential clients. This is where client relationships can be built and trust can be developed, and it must be a time-blocked focus of your commercial brokerage practice.

2. DIFFERENTIATION TO TURN A MEETING INTO A PRESENTATION OPPORTUNITY

So you got an appointment. Now you need a plan for uncovering critical information about the prospect. Throughout the conversion process, you want to make sure your time is spent with quality prospects who offer a strong probability of a completed transaction. In a shifted market, this invaluable information will primarily come from your first meeting and preparation beforehand. Your goal is to do the following:

- Do your pre-meeting due diligence.

- Uncover the prospect's real problems.

- Financially qualify the prospect.

- Ensure that the prospect has realistic expectations.

- Close for the solution presentation.

All the while, you must continue to differentiate yourself, relying on your solutions-oriented approach that is based on your specific knowledge and expertise.

Do your pre-meeting due diligence. While the most important information you need will be gleaned from your first meeting with a prospect, that doesn't mean you shouldn't arrive at the meeting armed with knowledge. You need to understand where to probe for pain, and research can reveal key pressure points. Do your due diligence: Explore their websites, google them and read the top media hits, explore public records (make sure you know who owns the property being discussed), and review any financial records available (Hoover's reports, filings with the SEC, etc.) to get a sense of the prospect's financial status. Look for those indicators of trouble that could help you direct the conversation, prove your worth to the prospect, and discover their value to you.

Uncover the prospect's real problems. While pre-meeting prep is important, the first face-to-face meeting with a client is where the magic happens. It's your opportunity to demonstrate your professional competencies and to differentiate yourself from other brokers they may be speaking to. It's easy to jump into why you're the best broker in town, but every broker will say that. Avoid the chest-beating of how great you are. High levels of anxiety, uncertainty, and risk aversion are common with prospects in a shifted market. You have to develop a relationship, let the truth of their situation unfold gradually. Differentiate yourself by showing concern about the prospect's problems and how your unique talents and skills will help them solve these problems. Instead of being the salesperson, present yourself as a professional consultant. Don't try to sell them, give them immediate solutions, or close too quickly.

Start the meeting with a brief introduction—who you are, what you do, and your specialties. Acknowledge the difficulties of the shifted market and the successes you've had despite them, particularly successes that might be of direct interest to the prospect: cutting occupancy costs, improving occupancy rates, developing deals based on creative financing, or whatever you believe the prospect might care about. Tell them a brief but engaging story of a past client who faced a situation similar to theirs.

Next, get them to open up. Spend most of the meeting asking open-ended questions that reveal their pain, such as the following:

1. *What have you been doing commercially over the last few years? –* You're looking for proven commercial activity.

2. *How's your current situation? –* You want them to discuss their business so that you understand the scope of or foundation of their issues better.

3. *What are your areas of concern? What problems have you been experiencing?* You're trying to get to the real problems here, something you can actually help them solve.

4. *Are you on the committee for making this decision for your company? Who else needs to be at our next meeting? –* Make sure you're dealing with a decision maker.

Wait for the answers to these or other questions. Don't underestimate the power of silence—it's only natural that they might hesitate to reveal difficult circumstances. For investors, it's probably that properties have been on the market for too long; for buyers, it's often that they can't find a property that meets their financial criteria. For tenants, they're concerned that they're paying too much in rent or they're swimming in space they don't need, and for landlords, it's vacant space. But there are unique nuances to every problem, and you need to understand all of them before you can develop a solution-based plan. If you can get a client to really open up to you, the hardest part of your conversion job is done, because the client has begun to trust you. It's proof that you've done your part to connect with their problem, that you've differentiated yourself, and that you are building rapport.

Financially qualify the prospect. While you're probing for problems, you also need to be asking questions that help you discover whether a transaction exists with the prospect in the near future. You have to use your seasoned broker's nose to "smell out" a real transaction from a dream transaction. One of the best ways to develop this sense is through experience, which is why it's important for new commercial brokers to work with seasoned veterans. Specifically, you need to determine if the prospect can actually complete a transaction. To do this, you will need to ask some hard questions. Don't be afraid to do so: These are the questions that can position you as an expert, that can differentiate you from your competition who are too desperate to qualify appropriately—who will take on any client, whether a transaction exists or not. You will need to do the following:

- Ask about their experience and track record with the type of transaction.

- If you are meeting with a buyer or investor, inquire about their financing arrangements up front, including specific details of available capital or agreements with lenders. Tell them that understanding their lender's requirements and restrictions will help you find the right property. Always follow through and check out their funding sources.

- If you are meeting with a tenant, inquire about their status and relationship with their current landlord, particularly any lease-related issues.

- And if you are meeting with a landlord, find out the strength and success of the current leasing team, whether it is internally marketed or through a third-party broker.

If a prospect hasn't purchased a building in years, has limited capital, is behind on their rent, or is otherwise financially unqualified, it may be best to move on to better prospects. For buyers in a shifted market, you need a stable of qualified, cash investors who can move quickly to take advantage of distressed situations. If they need assistance with creative financing options or need the owner to take back financing, it's crucial that you uncover this up front. Be sure that you have realistic expectations of earning a fee or a commission before converting the prospect to a client.

Ensure that the prospect has realistic expectations. In a shifted market, the biggest hurdle that brokers face is clients' unrealistic expectations—it seems that everybody has them. "Supposed" sellers are basing their expectations on market valuations from two or three years ago, and they will only sell for an amount that is unrealistic in the current market. These listings, no matter how tempting, will have very little chance of becoming closed transactions. Sometimes these sellers are in a negative equity situation (the loan is higher than the current valuation), creating a distressed property. We'll discuss these more in Tactic #12 Markets of the Moment.

Unrealistic buyers and tenants are looking for the deal of a lifetime. The dream of bargain-basement real estate prices brings out the unqualified buyers with no capital and very little chance of actually closing a transaction. You do *not* want to work with these people; they will waste your time and zap your energy.

> *Better to ask the tough questions up front. Too often, inexperienced agents delay asking the tough and sometimes obvious questions that they suspect may kill the deal because they are afraid of the answer. Ask them up front; better to find out the transaction won't happen early than spending a lot of your time and it falling apart later when you could have moved on to more productive business.*
>
> *David Neault,*
> *Norco, California*

It is the job of all commercial brokers to help establish realistic expectations with their clientele. This is a key opportunity to highlight your bona fides—you know the markets, what properties are trading for, current lease rates, true comparables, what concessions are being offered, etc. Exploring a prospect's expectations and finding out how open they are to the realities of the market are crucial during your meeting. Does the language prospects use match your knowledge of current real estate market conditions? Are they just out hunting for a bargain, or do they really understand what the investment requires? In a shifted market, it's often better to be the second or third broker to handle a property or client because the first broker spent six to twelve months breaking down the walls of unrealistic expectations. The client is now more prepared to accept the realities of the market. It's like the old joke goes: "first born, second wife, third Realtor."

Depending on what you discover about a prospect's expectations, this may be the point at which you decide that this individual is worth a greater investment of your time—or not.

Close for the solution presentation. After you've probed for pain and qualifying information, the close of the first meeting is where you need to give them the sizzle, not the steak. The steak is reserved for the solution presentation meeting. Show that you understand their problem with a quick recap: "It sounds like what you need to have happen is _____." This does two things: It demonstrates that you really were listening and you get confirmation of the core issue. Then share stories of how you've helped clients with that specific problem in the past. Leverage your expertise, your specialized knowledge, or your cobroker arrangement with a broker who specializes in the client's problem area. Tell the prospect something they likely don't know about the market. Show your passion for the market and the deal by talking in broad terms about what you would do— specifically, what other brokers might not. Highlight one creative approach you might take to solving their problem but save the actual specifics and details for the next meeting. I call this the solution presentation; you present a *detailed program of action* to accomplish the prospect's objective. Give them a first look at an accountability plan for how your firm will help them reach their goals. Drive the message home that by letting you handle the transaction, the prospect will save time and will make or save more money.

You can win their confidence if you remember that they are a person with a problem. Be counseling and relationship driven: You have to try to identify the problem and not just a possible transaction. In this way, you will convert them to a client for life.

Charles "Mac" McClure,
Dallas, Texas

This is your opportunity to truly differentiate yourself based on your market knowledge and expertise—you need to nail it. And don't leave until the next meeting—the solution presentation—is set and on the prospect's calendar. If you discover that you really can't help the prospect, or if they really won't need your services for some time and you've developed rapport, move them to your long-term lead cultivation list.

The passion you show for the project and for understanding their issues or concerns will move the conversation to the final stage: a solution presentation and a signed exclusive agreement.

3. DIFFERENTIATION TO GET FROM A SOLUTION PRESENTATION TO AN EXCLUSIVE AGREEMENT

In a shifting commercial market, uncertainties abound. Investors, tenants, and landlords *all* have a clouded, hazy, uncertain outlook. These potential clients are looking for decisive, confident leadership with their commercial real estate decisions. The successful broker will fill this void and demonstrate the ability to do so in the second meeting with a prospect, where they will offer their solution presentation and then close for an exclusive agreement.

After the first meeting, you have what you need to prepare a solution presentation for the prospect. On occasion, you can skip the first meeting because it is either a smaller transaction or you have a direct line to the decision makers and enough information (particularly through cultivation) to jump straight to preparing a presentation. Study your markets and your prospect's situation and do not be afraid to be bold and decisive in your assessments and decisions. This is how successful commercial brokers set themselves apart, especially in a shifted market.

At the meeting, begin with a short recap of the previous one to show that you have a clear understanding of the prospect's problem. Then dig into the specifics of what you will do to solve it. You must be specific: Explain exactly what you will do for the client to earn your commission and to help them solve their problems and achieve their objectives. Passive generalities won't cut it! The presentations should include detailed marketing plans, all avenues you will pursue to identify prospective buyers or tenants, how you will identify the best properties for a buyer or tenant, how often you will update them on your progress, what systems you have in place to make the process as smooth as possible, the team you have in place to support the transaction, and so on. Throughout, give more details of your experience and expertise, specifically as it relates to the client's transaction. Leverage the reputation of your brokerage as well.

If you're prepared to take your brokerage to the next level and earn money on the front and back end of every transaction, you need to think of yourself not just as an expert broker—a salesperson—but also as an expert marketer. Jeremy Cyrier, a CCIM instructor and the 2010 recipient of the Susan B. Groeneveld Award of Excellence from the CCIM Institute, made this shift, and his business has grown dramatically in the past year. His leads alone have quadrupled.

"I was tired of the same conversations with clients," said Jeremy. "Lead flow and deal flow were slow, but the 'what else can we be doing' conversation was increasing, quickly. Our model wasn't working." Jeremy took massive action and tore down his marketing platform, rebuilding it by asking the question, "Why would anyone wanting top dollar list their property right now?" When you're on a list, you're a commodity; this was Jeremy's revelation. You have few opportunities to differentiate yourself, which means you compete on price. Not ideal, particularly in a shift. His solution? Don't list—*position*. "I developed a marketing plan that offered clients the opportunity to position their properties, built on a belief that if their properties were unique, special, and different, people would want their property and might pay more for it."

Jeremy perused the database of lease-based properties to discover the information every prospect sees: addresses, space available, photos, brief descriptions, and prices. Every landlord was competing for attention based on generic pieces of information, and only price typically attracted attention. Jeremy broke down each category and discovered ways to position rather than list the property.

- **Photo** – Have the photo taken by a professional photographer (and never by a broker using a smart phone).

- **Address** – Most addresses are meaningless to prospects, other than indicating a neighborhood. Instead, name the property, like the John Hancock Tower in Boston, to give it prestige or to attract a certain type of tenant. For instance, if you want a tech company in the space, use a name like "Technology Innovation Place."

- **Space Available**: Don't just indicate the space available is "industrial for lease," "land for sale," or "office for lease"; use it like a headline to help you identify the ideal tenant and then leverage that information in how you position the property. Headlines like "Skip the Commute – First Floor Office Space (office for lease)" and "Attention Architects, Attorneys, and Tech Firms – Cambridge Office Space! (office for lease)" get better results.

- **Brief Description** – Don't be generic. Use the limited space to highlight what's most compelling about the property.

- **Price** – If you get everything else right, price is a nonissue. "In fact," said Jeremy, "after changing these elements for new properties we've taken on, we've actually raised the price and had more interest than when the price was lower."

What Jeremy's approach offers is a clientcentric approach to marketing: "You have to get into the client's mind, hook into something they already know, and use that to *position* the property." And that approach has dramatically improved his client list and his success with transactions. "For one property, in the brief description, which was something like 'office space for lease in Cambridge,' we changed it to say that the property offered easy access to Harvard and Cambridge and that it had housed some very successful technology companies, which we named. Within a week, people started calling us and reading it back to us, saying, 'I own a technology company and need access to the talent at MIT and Harvard, and I want to be in a building where businesses have been successful.' It was amazing."

Jeremy now gets paid up-front fees by clients for his marketing efforts, which he can easily ask for once he's mapped out his creative and proactive approach and his success rate with other properties. A marketing company doesn't front the money to help clients; you shouldn't either. And he gets a commission on the back end when the transaction closes as well.

Regardless of your approach, you want to present a clear road map to a closed transaction for the client. More than anything, the presentation must highlight your creativity, your proactive efforts. The client inherently understands that in a shifted market, that will be the only way to get deals done. Gone are the days of advertising listings and waiting for the calls to come in. You have to make deals happen. Show the client you have the expertise, the drive, and the creativity to do so. Your clients will appreciate your clarity of thought and decisive actions.

At the end of your solution presentation, close for an exclusive agreement. "Commercial real estate is a business of control," explains Paige Aiken, a commercial broker in Atlanta, Georgia. "You either have control or you have *nothing*. Your goal is to be your clients' exclusive representation as a listing agent, buyer representative, or tenant representative. You have to control the inventory: both properties and the people you represent. The purpose of getting control is to close transactions—always be working toward this end goal. Brokers that control the inventory or the tenants get paid. Brokers that don't, don't."

> *Focus on the overall business strategy of the client—not just on the transaction. We should be guiding and advising our customers, not just selling to them.*
> *Brock Danielson,*
> *Phoenix, Arizona*

The key to obtaining an exclusive agreement is convincing the client that it's in their best interest to work with a broker on an exclusive basis, and that broker should be you because you are prepared to be held accountable for your results. Prospects could not care less that exclusive agreements work better for you or that this is how you do business. They simply want the best possible way to solve their problem or reach their objective. Convince them it is better to work with "one" totally accountable broker and get 110 percent of their effort than to work with five totally unaccountable brokers and get 10 percent effort from each. Explain to them that with an exclusive agreement, the odds of getting a deal done are greatly enhanced.

To back up these statements, you must prove your ability to get deals done and that starts with building trust. *To get trust, you must first give it.* When I was working to get clients to sign an exclusive agreement, I would guarantee the commission on the transaction—proof of my commitment to the transaction and proof of my confidence in getting it done right. The exclusive agreement would clearly state a proposed commission, but it would also indicate that the final commission to be paid was at the discretion of the client and would be based on my performance. "Mr. Prospect," I would say, "this is your guarantee that I will perform. If I don't perform to your expectations, you can access all or part of the real estate commission." You might think this is a dangerous game to play, particularly when every dollar you earn will be hard-fought. But I never once had a client access the fees. By first demonstrating to a prospect that I trusted them to be fair and honorable with the commission, they then would trust me to make sure the deal got done right and sign the exclusive agreement. Trust given was trust gained.

Roger Staubach of the Staubach Company once had a presentation with a large corporate prospect. The CFO complained that the real estate fee was more than he made in a year. Kevin Hayes, a senior broker working with Roger, said, "If we don't save you at least four times our fees, we'll give you up to 100 percent of the commission." Roger was shocked at the time. But they got the assignment, closed the transaction, and saved the client more than the promised amount of money, thus more than earning the full commission. From that point on, all brokers at the Staubach Company had to have value-add proposition guarantees in all their exclusive agreements.

Another way to prove accountability and your drive to be hyper-proactive is to set a time limit for the agreement and include a simple cancellation clause. Butch and Rhonda West of Austin, Texas, and Kyle Drake of Houston, Texas, took on a property that had been on the market for some time. They boldly told the owner, "We will sell this property in sixty days. If we don't, you are free to fire us." Honestly, what's the worst that will happen if you make a commitment like this? You'll get fired. In a shifted market, that may happen more often anyway. This isn't the type of offer you would make to all of your clients, but in some situations it may be appropriate, particularly if a potential client is gun-shy; and it's a unique way to differentiate yourself from your competition. Butch, Rhonda, and Kyle performed, got an offer on the property in sixty days, and closed a $10-million-dollar transaction.

No matter how you do it, always go for an exclusive agreement. Aside from the greater guarantee of income, an exclusive can be the first step in a long-term relationship by allowing you to focus your energy on the true interests of your client, and thus building trust. An exclusive can also be used to make effective business development calls on prospects or owners. By controlling one property or prospect in a specific market area, you gain unmatched access to information and firsthand knowledge of market conditions that you can leverage with other prospects in that market. Success begets success; clients beget new clients.

In a shifted market, every viable prospect, every appointment, and every opportunity to get to an exclusive agreement is precious and worth every minute you spend throughout the conversion process. Yes, you'll spend time on the phone with unqualified prospects, you'll go to meetings that lead nowhere, you'll put in a lot of work and never get an agreement. But sometimes you will. And those "sometimes" make all the other times worth it; they keep your business alive. So pick up the phone daily and ask somebody for a meeting—and then show them what you're capable of.

TACTIC #6
CATCH PEOPLE IN YOUR WEB –
INTERNET LEAD CONVERSION

Innovation is the specific instrument of entrepreneurship.
The act that endows resources with a new capacity to create wealth.
PETER F. DRUCKER

In the area of Internet-based prospecting and marketing, there is little doubt that our residential brethren have embraced the Internet to a far greater extent and with far greater success than our commercial colleagues. Online MLS listings specifically changed the game for residential agents. According to the *2010 National Association of Realtors Profile of Home Buyers and Sellers*, 89 percent of home buyers used the Internet in their search for a home. Residential agents had no choice but to move their efforts online, and the shifted commercial market is now bringing this same level of urgency to our business.

Before you say, "Yes, but that's residential; commercial is different," let me tell you that the game is definitely changing for commercial agents. Buyers and sellers are rapidly migrating online, particularly as they try to stay informed about the shifting market. Need proof? Ben Kinney, tech leader and CEO of the top real estate team in Bellingham, Washington, shared that a broker on his Seattle team recently wrote an offer on a $67-million-dollar commercial property. That offer came through his posting on Craigslist, a site many view as the online equivalent of a yard sale.

What was once a referral-driven business is now changing. Ben Kinney has watched this happen with his own business. "If a prospect doesn't have a referral, they base their decision on the information they have on hand. This might initially be signs and marketing materials, but they will soon likely go online. Once there, the person they see the most is the person they'll probably decide to hire." Ben has ramped up his Internet prospecting, marketing, and conversion efforts over the past three years, and now about one-third of his business comes through his online lead generation efforts.

In a shifted market, when appointments are hard to come by and transactions are even rarer, you need more leads than ever before. So why would you not use every possible opportunity to connect with prospects and clients, to generate more leads, and to convert them? Today, you have no choice but to be online. The challenge for most commercial brokers is that "being online" seems to be a new concept that only techies can grasp or one that is overwhelming considering the vastness of the online universe. It requires time, money, and resources that are in scarce supply and from which you are demanding a measurable return on investment. But let me repeat: *You have no choice*! You have to go where your prospects and clients are—if they aren't finding you online, you can be sure they'll find somebody else.

The good news is that the sheer number of residential agents who adopted online strategies in recent years has both driven a lot of industry-specific innovation and, more importantly, driven massive investments to make these tools accessible to tech novices. Ramping up is not nearly as difficult as it was just a few years ago. Once you have a system in place, it will continue to work for you twenty-four hours a day, seven days a week.

INTERNET LEAD GENERATION AND CONVERSION

Figure 14

Surprisingly, today's tech tools aren't simply about generating leads; be prepared to expand your thinking as you explore the power of the Internet in lead conversion. The number of commercial brokers maximizing their use of online tactics is still small, so race ahead of your competition and show your clients that you are a leader in the market.

When building and leveraging an effective online presence, you'll have three primary areas of focus comprising this tactic (see figure 14). First, you have to build your online presence. This begins with identifying your brand and ends with a strategic selection of Internet and social media sites that support it. Second, you'll proactively market your listings and services to drive traffic and generate leads. Lastly, you'll purposefully capture and convert those leads by leveraging the same offer-response strategies you already use every day offline when talking to potential clients.

Considering that entire books have been written on the topics covered in this tactic, we can only begin to scratch the surface here. Nevertheless, this chapter is longer than most and every paragraph is packed with advice and tips. Get ready to start taking notes because we firmly believe that if you don't immediately master these tactics, your competition will. Additionally, Ben Kinney and my coauthor, Jay Papasan, created an excellent real estate-specific resource, *Soci@l: Attract Friends, Followers, and Connections to Your Business*, which offers valuable insights for the development of this tactic. I encourage you to read it for more how-to direction for social media efforts, especially if you are just getting started. You can download it for free at www.socialthebook.com.

Before we begin, it's important to remember one of my favorite Gary Keller truisms: People tend to overestimate the short-term impact of innovation while underestimating the long-term impact. If you have a minimal online presence right now, don't expect to start converting a massive number of leads next week. It takes time to ramp up and become visible. However, over time you'll likely be surprised by the cumulative impact these tactics can have on your brokerage. At the end of the day, we believe this tactic is perhaps the greatest opportunity for you to differentiate your commercial practice in this fiercely competitive and shifting commercial marketplace.

1. BUILD AND MAINTAIN YOUR ONLINE PRESENCE

Running before learning to walk: a common problem in our technolgy-enhanced world. We learn just enough to get ourselves into trouble, and suddenly our online presence has spun out of control. We'll help you avoid that trap by exploring how you build your online brand, identifying what's already out there and then clarifying what it is you want to communicate—how you want to differentiate yourself. With your brand firmly in hand, we'll then walk you through a strategic approach to presenting that brand online—you'll build your online presence, first through your website and then through social networking sites.

Build your online brand. At a seminar on social media strategy not long ago, Jason Seiden of Ajax Social Media asked the participants to google themselves to understand what their clients or potential clients see. While you might think that a group of professionals would have a fairly clear picture of their online presence, many were shocked by what they found. One in particular got a rude awakening from his online image. Among the first search results was a quote from his college newspaper in which he declared, "I joined a fraternity to get ____." He was mortified. And how do you think this affected his image with his potential clients?

This story, while extreme, isn't unique—it happens to all of us. Collegiate foolhardiness aside, we have little control over what others post online about us—a reality that is a thorn in the side of many businesses not yet engaged with their customers online or proactive in their approach. In an age of smartphones and social media—when everything we do or say is just a click, post, or snapshot away from being shared online—today's commercial broker needs to have a clear online brand-building strategy.

Do you have an online brand? The answer is yes, you do. You may not have a brand that you've cultivated, but there is likely a wealth of information about you available online—some of which you would want prospects to know, some of which you wouldn't. So begin your brand-building efforts with a brand audit. Google yourself and click through the links that come up. Pay close attention to the initial search results, but also take the time to dig deep. Review your LinkedIn, Facebook, and other social media pages and view them as others view them.

As you go, answer these questions:

- Where are you being found online?

- Would a client searching for you find basic, accurate contact information to be able to connect with you offline?

- What information is out there?

- Do you have the ability to edit or delete the information?

- Does your online world accurately reflect your offline brand-building efforts?

- Based on what's out there, do you seem to be an established, credible expert?

Hopefully, everything you find corresponds with the professional brand you've embraced. If you don't find much (your online presence is minimal) or what you find isn't flattering (your online presence is mixed), don't sweat it. A little conscious effort can quickly update your brand, improve it, and eventually drive any unwanted results you aren't able to delete so far down in the search results that they become innocuous.

Many rush into the Internet space with a great sense of urgency but little forethought. They build impressive websites and social media presences, but because they didn't begin with the brand in mind, the best they can hope to achieve are substandard results and the worst is a hodgepodge of ideas which can actually drive away potential clients. Take the time to develop a firm grasp of your professional brand before expanding your online presence. Remember, the essence of any broker's brand, online and off, should be expertise—one of the key ways to differentiate yourself from your competitors, as we discussed earlier in Tactic #5. Using your brand message as a foundation will help you be consistent in your differentiation efforts across multiple platforms.

But you must also consider other aspects of your brand beyond the purely professional. Who are you as a person, and therefore as a broker? What is your personality and which aspects do you want to leverage as part of your brand? We've discussed the importance of building personal relationships and rapport in the previous tactics—you can do that with your online brand as well. Do you want to emphasize integrity, your professional approach, your education? Or are you known as the friendly, laid-back broker with charisma who knows how to get things done? You should be just as consistent in these messages as in all other aspects of your brand.

Over time, to protect the brand you're building, you'll want to use tools like Google Alerts or TweetBeep to stay informed when people write about you, blog about you, tweet about you, and so on. They also help you stay informed about how your name and brand are being used online. If you find that you're getting negative attention for any reason or that you are being confused online with somebody else, do not ignore it! Be proactive, respond quickly, and then find a way to fix the problem.

THE DO'S AND DON'TS OF ONLINE BRANDING

DO

- Include your logo, business name, and website on all your online profiles.

- Match your online image to your ideal clientele through all mediums including images, text, and video.

- Insert personality into both your business and personal profiles. We are still in an industry where the majority of people choose to do business with you because they like or can relate to you.

DON'T

- Disclose information, including personal facts, anywhere online that you wouldn't want a potential client to read.

- Post exclusively about listings and real estate-related subjects on your profiles. Your audience may start to ignore your messages, or, even on the extreme, block or remove your updates.

- Disclose personal information that might endanger your family or yourself, including photos of young children or photos that might show a home address or a notable landmark.

- Participate in conversations or start ones that might offend your audience, including political, religious, or social issues, unless you are prepared for the consequences.

Figure 15 (Source: *Soci@l*)

Reputation is one of the top reasons clients choose to work with a broker. Make sure you have a clear idea of your brand and nip brand attacks in the bud.

Create your online presence, starting with your website.

Building expertise is ultimately about one thing: delivering content your prospects and clients want and need—properties for sale or lease, property valuations, market information, and guidance on the buying, selling, and leasing processes. Your primary platform for delivering that content is your website.

Your Website: The Center of Your Web

Figure 16

The heart of your online presence will be your brokerage website. We're talking about the site that represents your personal business, not a national or regional company website that happens to feature your bio. The distinction is important. First, you want control of the content, and second, you want control of the leads. Your website is your *lead capture engine*—the center of your Web—and you'll drive as many potential clients to it as possible as you expand your online presence.

FIVE STRATEGIES FOR DEVELOPING
A CREDIBLE WEBSITE

1. Recognize that your website should be more than a business card—it should reflect your brand-building efforts and become the focus of your online (and often offline) lead generation efforts.

2. Offer properties, properties, and more properties. It's the number one reason real estate consumers search online.

3. Offer content: information, education, and opportunities. Quality content reflects your expertise and provides reasons for prospects to contact you (for example, invite them to register for a special report on renegotiating a commercial lease or a list of "best buys").

4. Present multiple ways for visitors to contact you to capture leads. Capture, capture, capture!

5. Include links to all your online activities. Curate your online presence by directing them to the places you want to be found.

Figure 17

The holy grail of real estate is access to property information. Survey after survey confirms that the top reason potential clients visit a real estate website is to look at properties. While residential agents have mature MLS and Internet Data Exchange (IDX) systems, equivalent services in our commercial industry are basically in their infancy. But Commercial Information Exchanges (CIEs) have been established in a number of markets and are currently expanding. Your objective is to give prospects who visit your site sufficient reasons to register to access these listings.

After property information, buyers may be looking for shift-specific information on buying investment properties, the commercial buying process, or simply making the most of their real estate dollars. Tenants may be searching for content on exiting or renegotiating leases, selecting retail locations, or negotiating build-out. What sellers and landlords want is information about the market and ideas for maximizing their ROI or NOI by taking advantage of market trends. Here's a tip: If you aren't sure what kind of information your clients might want, spend some time in the Sent folder of your email. It won't take long to see the kinds of questions they're asking, and you may already have most of the content you need for your website in the responses you've emailed over the past few months.

Of course, if you don't give visitors a path to connect with you, your efforts are pointless. To convert as many leads as possible, give them multiple opportunities to connect with you: forms, phone, email, text, carrier pigeons—whatever you have available. While online forms are a great way to capture information, don't restrict access based on what's best for you. You'll miss out on leads who aren't ready to share that much information. We'll discuss this in more detail later in this tactic.

Broadcast your online presence. Include links to all of your social media resources, both as a way to connect and as another option to access your content.

Just remember that property listings come first—in survey after survey, it's consistently the number one reason potential buyers and tenants search the Web. If potential clients visit your website to see listings, you then get additional opportunities to provide value and connect. You can offer a link to an area information guide for out-of-town prospects. Offer a no-obligation property evaluation for sellers and landlords who want to know the market value of their properties. Provide links to various resources based on your visitors' interests. It's that simple: If you offer people what they really want and present credible content, you are furthering your brand and reputation. Your website will become a trusted resource and you will garner name recognition and recall.

Expand your online presence through social networking sites. Today's top Internet brokers have extended their online presence beyond the traditional boundaries of their brokerage website and now put substantial effort into building their brand on networking and social media sites. You need both to reach your target audiences, and together they communicate your brand message (see figure 18).

For most brokers, their sphere is vital for referrals and repeat business. Social media is an opportunity to build deeper relationships with your most important advocates and people of influence within your communities. Prospecting for buyers and sellers or interacting with huge audiences are strategies that scale extremely well online. And blogging is a proven method for increasing your visibility on search engines and helping buyers and sellers find your business. The challenge with all of these is they require regular effort and attention to be effective.

The important thing to consider is that you must establish a presence in line with your brand, and you need to decide how deep you want to go to make the best use of your time. Following are the top networks we recommend based on traffic and ease of use.

Your Online Presence

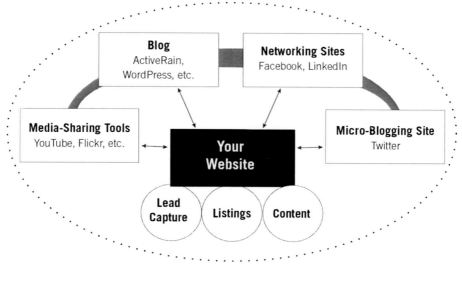

Figure 18

TOP SOCIAL NETWORKS FOR DEVELOPING YOUR ONLINE PRESENCE

1. **Facebook**: Google+ may be the new kid on the block, but Facebook, with more than 600 million users, is still the undisputed king of the social media hill. While many people use it simply to socialize with friends and family, many others use it to learn about products, to learn more about companies (particularly those with fan pages), to research professionals, or to position themselves as experts. Facebook combines the best of media sharing, microblogging, and networking on one platform. It can be a primary tool for brokers to stay connected with their core clients and sphere.

2. **LinkedIn**: While people may not search it to find a broker, a LinkedIn page is one of the first items that will come up in a Google search for your name, making it prime brand-building territory. And as a business networking site, it should be your go-to tool for connecting with your industry network and communities. Besides updating your picture and profile, one of the most powerful things you can do is ask for (and give) client recommendations. Not only will it make a great first impression on potential brokerage clients, it is also a reason to connect with past clients to ask for referrals or repeat business.

3. **YouTube**: The definitive video-sharing website, YouTube is the second most popular social media site. You may not think of yourself as a video star, but having your own YouTube channel can be a powerful way to increase visibility. Short, informative videos help you build credibility, offer information prospects might be seeking, and bring life and energy to your brand. Plug videos into your website, substitute them for blog entries ... even ask current and past clients for testimonials.

4. **Blogs**: WordPress is an easy out-of-the-box solution for most blogging needs. Blogging itself is one of the primary ways you can build content on the Web that over time will help make you increasingly visible through search engines. Take a long look at real estate-specific blog platforms like ActiveRain. With more than 150,000 members and a million-plus pages of content, no other social media site does more to help real estate buyers and sellers input "long tail" search terms— those with longevity—and connect with the brokers who specialize in them.

5. **Twitter**: An excellent way to touch those in your network frequently and unobtrusively, Twitter is the master platform for microblogging: It enables almost real-time conversations on a massive scale. Despite a confounding 140-character limit on communications, Twitter presents you with an opportunity to stay top of mind with those in your network and to position yourself as an expert by offering current tips and information. While it may not be ideal for lead generation, it can be leveraged effectively for broker-to-broker referrals and driving traffic to your blog.

"Online social networks are most useful when they address real failures in the operation of offline networks," said Professor Mikolaj Jan Piskorski in the *Working Knowledge* newsletter from Harvard Business School (September 14, 2009). Today, they play that role better than ever. Recent spectacular growth in social media has lead to greater integration, and while this is a bit disturbing to some, it offers opportunities to those who are paying attention. You can connect your LinkedIn profile to your Facebook page to your YouTube channel to your Twitter feed to your website—the hub of all activity—to present a holistic picture of who you are and what you have to offer. And sending a consistent message has never been easier with free tools like TweetDeck and HootSuite, which allow you to manage all of your social media from one central site, posting the same content to all with the click of a few buttons.

A mistake that many professionals make is trying to keep their online personal and professional lives separate. Jason Seiden coined the term "profersonal" to describe the true, integrated state of our online worlds—and increasingly, our offline ones. While I don't recommend that you share pictures of your kids with all of your clients, you can't expect that clients won't find your personal pages or request a connection through them. Search engines won't differentiate between your personal and professional pages, sites, or profiles, and it's unlikely that clients or prospects will either. Rather than try to create barriers that are ineffective, you may need to use just one page or account and leverage privacy settings and group options to share the information you want to share with the people you want to share it with.

As you develop your brand-building strategy, ask yourself this question: "How far am I willing to go?" If you plan to invest serious time and resources to develop a broad platform, that's great. But equally valuable to your business is using scarce resources to cover the basics—your website, Facebook page, and LinkedIn profile should be your minimum. You don't have to have a YouTube channel or a daily blog to be visible to the people you want to reach, but those efforts could certainly improve your search engine ranking. If you have resources but limited time, seek out professionals at any level to help develop content. Ben Kinney paid college students $20 to write blog articles, which he would outline for them and then review to ensure they properly reflected his brand. Kristan Cole, of Wasilla, Alaska, pays just a few hundred dollars a month for a professional service to manage her blog, which attracts readers statewide as well as buyers making inquiries from all over.

Be smart, leverage your team to get the basics covered as quickly as possible, and then build from there.

2. MARKET LISTINGS AND SERVICES FOR LEAD GENERATION

Building an online brand is one thing; attracting potential clients or buyers and lessors is another. Even the best brands need a focused marketing plan that aligns with the tools and content offered if they are going to do their job: generate more converted leads and income.

As you develop a plan to market your services and listings, first ask, "Where is my target audience?" Consider who it is you are trying to reach. Ask your clients and your network where they find information on brokers, properties, or the real estate market. Research your competitors and find out where they are online. Look at statistics on web traffic. Read reports from trend-watchers such as Stefan Swanepoel, a bestselling author who publishes reports on real estate trends as well as social media ones. Because opportunities for getting in the path of your potential clients are vast, this research is critical to a targeted use of your resources.

Kristan Cole heard about a property that a local bank was having trouble with because it was in a remote community where there are no commercial agents, so she stepped in and offered to assist. When she visited the remote community, she realized that the normal channels for marketing the property would not work. "So, I went to the library and to city officials and asked how people communicated out here in the Aleutian Islands. A young man at the library indicated that there was a local website that everyone used to communicate interest in buying and selling properties. I created an ad for the property and had it posted on this site (similar to Craigslist). A buyer out of Washington State saw the ad and emailed me." All it took was a bit of research to discover where she needed to be online to get a property sold.

If your audience resides in a special online community, great. More than likely, though, your audience is scattered across the Web, particularly as you try to expand your possible targets to generate more leads. Figure 19 shows the interaction between your brand-building and marketing efforts.

Marketing Listings and Services Online

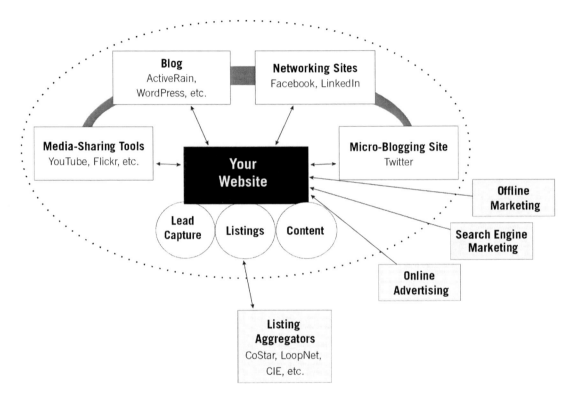

Figure 19

To effectively, efficiently, and quickly leverage your resources online, follow the priority list in figure 20 for your online marketing efforts.

TOP FOUR ONLINE MARKETING TACTICS

1. Paid search engine marketing
2. Craigslist
3. Listing aggregators
4. Organic search engine marketing

Figure 20

1. Paid search engine marketing. This is simply paying for pay-per-click or other types of ads on search engines. When somebody in your geographic area types in a key word term that you've purchased an ad for, your ad shows up at the top of the results or off to the side of the page. While this requires an investment, pay-per-click ads can be very affordable because you only pay for the ad when people click through. If they don't click through (say they see the ad, but contact you directly), you don't pay. The best part is that the result is instantaneous. Unlike organic search engine marketing efforts, which can take months to build up a head of steam, you can get instant results here. And because the feedback is immediate, you can adjust your tactics daily (tweaking the key words like "commercial properties [your market]" and the amount you're willing to pay per click) until you find the sweet spot. It's that simple.

Similar to the search engine pay-per-click ads are ads you can purchase on some social media sites, such as Facebook. These ads present an opportunity to target people in a certain industry, in a certain geographical area ... even a certain company. They can be very effective when you are trying to break into a certain niche or specialization, but can be equally effective if you are trying to sell a property that might meet the needs of specialty buyers.

Again, *Soci@l* provides a great tutorial on creating and targeting pay-per-click ads; however, it's really simple: Just go to www.facebook.com/advertising and follow the cues. You can target by demographics, geography, and even down to specific companies. For instance, if you had a property that would be perfect for a specific company (say an autoparts store) and you knew where the company headquarters was located (say AutoZone in Memphis, Tennessee) you could create an ad for "Ideal Consumer Automotive Outlet Locations!" that would appear on those employees' screens whenever they were on Facebook.

2. Craigslist. I've already told you the amazing story about the $67 million Craigslist lead, but that was just one spectacular example. Craigslist isn't the site you once knew, full of used sofas and strange personal ads—it has matured and was recently ranked the tenth most-visited website in the United States. If you discount it, if you think that your clientele would never use it, you are probably wrong. Companies—from startups to mom-and-pops to national corporations—use Craigslist to find talent, to find outsourced resources, and more. It's not much of a leap for them to look for real estate or real estate professionals while they are already on the site. Post every listing on Craigslist. It's an affordable way to reach a broader audience.

The challenge with Craigslist is that, in most markets, there is already plenty of competition. With lots of properties being posted, your ads may only appear on the first page of results for minutes, not hours. Of course, many people will simply search Craigslist for specific key words related to what they need. Still, you may need to experiment with the timing of your posts to get the best results. Craigslist will also flag listings that are being reposted repeatedly, so brokers who are serious about this marketing method will typically create three to five variations on a listing ad and leverage assistants (virtual or staff) or software to switch them out throughout the day. On the residential side, this is such an effective way to get the phone to ring that top brokers are not only advertising their own listings, they are also getting permission to advertise other brokers' listings. The more ads, the better.

3. Listing aggregators. CoStar and LoopNet are the two main listing aggregators for the commercial real estate industry. There is no better way to attain broad visibility for your listings than by leveraging these services. If you put the same thought and effort into showcasing your properties on these sites (rich descriptions and professional-quality photos) that you would invest in an expensive magazine ad, you'll get much better results.

4. Organic search engine marketing. Search engines are consistently the hub of website traffic, with 68 percent of all searches passing through the Google portal, according to a recent Hitwise report. While paid marketing can offer more immediate results, in the long term, organic marketing can offer better results. But again, it is a long-term strategy because it depends upon leveraging your activity on your website and elsewhere.

The goal of organic marketing is to target all of your efforts and use search engine optimization techniques to increase the visibility of your online offerings as your targets search for certain key words on search engine sites. Search engines continually scour websites for content and rank them for validity. To rank "organically" is to be visible and deemed important by a search engine for a particular search phrase, like "commercial real estate Boston." Being on the first page of Google results when somebody searches for the term "commercial real estate" in your area is a fantastic achievement, but a difficult one to achieve. You have to tailor your existing online content to your search criteria (usually specific key words entered into search engines), as well as produce regular, new content associated with those same key words. Here are some simple things you can do to improve your visibility.

- Integrate key words and phrases on your website (including the metadata, if you know how) and your other online activities.

- Expand the content on your website.

- And, of course, start a blog.

Begin by making a list of twenty-five words and phrases that prospects might use to search for properties or services that you offer. Consider the obvious, such as "City Name + Commercial Real Estate," but you must go further. All your competitors will be competing for the same common key word searches, which can make them both the most expensive (in terms of money and effort) and the least productive. Think of key words associated with industries, neighborhoods, and communities that commercial clients might use to refine their searches. The goal is to identify the "long tail" search terms that tend to be the least competitive and the most productive.

Chris Anderson, editor of *Wired* and author of *The Long Tail*, presented a theory that for online retailers, given a near unlimited variety of products, the most popular items would produce only about 20 percent of the revenue while all the others would comprise 80 percent. Bricks-and-mortar stores are forced to focus on the most popular items because they only have so much shelf space. Internet companies, like Netflix, Amazon.com, and, honestly, any real estate brokerage, have no constraints on inventory and get to enjoy the benefits of marketing the "long tail" inventory. This isn't just theory; it plays out in real life. In an experiment detailed in *Soci@l*, the authors found that, generally speaking, about 80 percent of their online real estate traffic was generated by long-tail search terms and 20 percent was generated by the top key words. So dig deep and make sure you are focusing on more than just the most obvious commercial real estate key words. You may want to find a thorough resource on search engine optimization as well as read *Soci@l* cover to cover to best leverage the key words you identify.

Opportunities to leverage key words are easier to come by if you offer more content on your website. And offering more content improves the validity of your site. Consider your areas of specialization and your efforts at differentiating yourself in your market and provide content in line with those two factors. Update your content, even if you aren't writing a blog—keep it as fresh as possible. Offer tutorials, calculators, and other tools that prospects might be looking for (in addition to listings, of course).

One of the best things you can do to improve your organic ranking with search engines is to write a blog and post new content frequently. ActiveRain is a great tool for real estate professionals who want to create blogs, but there are other easy-to-use blog platforms out there too, like WordPress or TypePad. Blogging takes time and effort, and blogs that go dark for months or even weeks on end are almost completely useless. So don't head down this path unless you're serious about devoting the time to keeping up with it. The wonderful thing about blogs is that they are interactive: You can track responses to your content and identify topics that strike a chord or trends that may be emerging in your market. Kristan Cole's web content vendor scours the news wires for commercial real estate stories and creates regular, key word-driven content for her Alaska Real Estate blog. So your commitment is relative—your blog needs to have consistent, quality content posts, but you don't have to do it all (or any of it) by yourself. That said, you need to be supervising the messages and staying connected to make sure that your team is promoting the right brand.

Overall, improving your search engine ranking is a useful strategy, but if you expect great results for minimal effort, you will be disappointed. It takes time, effort, and sometimes money to build high visibility organically.

We can't end this discussion without two important reminders: First, if you hesitate to invest in Internet strategies because you aren't particularly tech savvy, many professionals are ready, willing, and able to help you. Professional writers help clients create blogs, web developers can help you determine the easiest way to set up a website that meets your needs, some web companies offer both development services and strategy consultation, and marketers now specialize in search engine optimization and online platform development. If you need help, it's out there.

Second, your offline marketing efforts should be well-integrated with your online efforts. In all of your offline communication, promote your webpages or profiles and anything you offer on your site that may interest your prospects, such as free content, special calculators, information they can sign up to receive, etc. Your signs and business cards should include your web address, and when appropriate, invite potential buyers to see space plans or pro formas that might be of interest. In your online marketing, particularly on your website, mention your offline activities, such as speeches you might be giving, events you might be hosting, etc.

Every Friday, I send out "Larry's Deal of the Week" to my interested buyers. These may be properties that I am representing, or they may be properties from another broker. It doesn't matter—as long as my clients know that I am going to bring them the best deals on the best properties in this market, and I have an opportunity to cultivate their business on a regular basis.

Larry Culbertson,
Atlanta, Georgia

Remember, your goal is to drive traffic to your website, because once a visitor lands there, you can capture them.

3. CAPTURE AND CONVERT LEADS

All of the web traffic in the world is meaningless if you don't know who has visited. If you can't follow up, it's not a lead—it's just a number in a list of website hits. And if you can't follow up, you can't convert your online efforts into appointments, clients, and closed transactions.

Capture, capture, capture! Capturing leads that you can convert is the most important outcome of your online efforts. In fact, it's the only outcome you should care about. If your website is not capturing leads, it's nothing more than an expensive business card.

On your website, you must present offers that would entice a visitor to give you their contact information. During our research, we conducted a rough study of lead capture. We randomly selected twenty-five residential agent websites and twenty-five commercial broker websites. When we visited the residential agent sites, we found that all of them made an offer of some kind and requested our contact information. The commercial broker websites? *Fewer than five made an offer or requested contact information.*

We suspect that commercial brokers are wary of seeming overly aggressive or unsophisticated. Essentially, they aren't thinking about the offer as the basis of capture. You have something your prospects want: expertise. So leverage it. Ask yourself, "What is it my prospects want enough that they would be willing to give me their contact information to receive?" Maybe it's a free customized report based on their property requirements. Maybe it's access to your weekly *Ten Best Deals* newsletter. Maybe it's access to advanced property search options if you have a more developed site for presenting listings. Maybe it's a free valuation of their property. You are an expert and you possess market knowledge—leverage that to entice people into your database. Canadian broker Benjamin Bach, of Kitchener, Ontario, makes three prominent offers to connect on the homepage of his website: Get the property hotlist, come to a class, and meet me at Starbucks. These serve to capture cool, warm, and hot leads for his brokerage.

The simplest form of capture is having three little boxes on your website with the invitation, "Enter your name, phone number, and email address to learn more." The information entered can be emailed to you or added directly to a database. While a web professional can help you develop a much more sophisticated capture system using forms of various complexity, if you do not at least have this level of capture on your website, the Internet is still a vast, untapped resource.

You can also capture visitors by asking them to connect with you on LinkedIn or Facebook, or by asking them to contact you in any way they prefer. Present them with multiple options for interacting with you online and off. Understand that Internet consumers each prefer to communicate in their own way—email, text, social media, face-to-face, or even by knocking on the door—and that may not be the way that you prefer. Just keep reminding yourself, "If I don't capture, I can't convert."

Convert leads with massive action. Multiple communication avenues is important to engaging and connecting with prospects, but it is the very essence of your conversion process. People are more guarded in some forms of communication than in others, particularly in email and by phone, as those two methods are the most fraught with spam or telemarketers. "It's going to take trying each way of communicating with each lead to find out what works best with them. If you don't, you could be missing out on massive lead conversion opportunities." Ben Kinney calls this massive action the "Ten Days of Pain" approach to conversion. His group contacts the prospect every day via different methods for ten consecutive days. A National Association of Realtors study indicated many choose their broker within fourteen days of initiating their search, so Ben hedges and tries to convert as many Internet leads to appointments as possible in the first ten days.

Path of Online Conversion

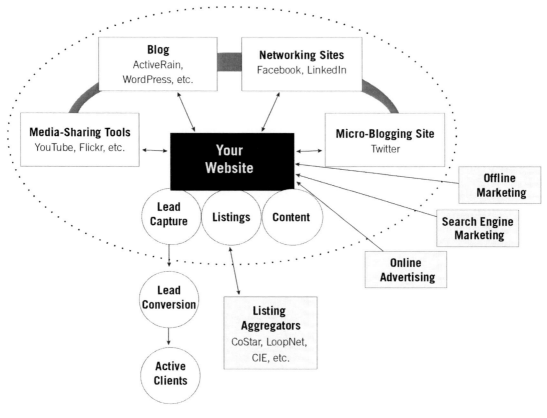

Figure 21

This is just one approach to the kind of ambitious and aggressive follow-up necessary to convert leads in a shifted market. It can seem overwhelming, but it is highly effective and no one ever complains. If anything, once they connect, clients compliment his team on their incredible persistence and tenacity. The following are seven ways you too can shift your Internet lead conversion efforts into a higher gear.

1. **Leverage your team**. If you have a support team in place, you don't need to be the first responder to Internet leads. If possible, the first response should be autogenerated so that it happens within minutes: This is just a simple message that lets them know when a real person will be in touch, which should preferably happen immediately and certainly within the first twenty-four hours. The second response can be more detailed but still scripted and can be delivered by your executive assistant, a paid prospector, a junior broker, or even a virtual assistant. Use your team to lay the groundwork. Develop clear processes and scripts for how and when to follow up with different types of leads generated online.

2. **Do one minute of research.** Today, despite our concerns about online privacy, you can find an amazing amount of information with simple, affordable tools. If all you have is an email address (which is usually the case), you can still connect with prospects in a variety of ways. Take their email and name (if provided) and execute a simple Google search. This is usually enough to find someone's social media and other pages. Xobni (inbox backward) is an Outlook add-on that does the same process at a more sophisticated level: It can identify any accounts associated with an email on Facebook, LinkedIn, Twitter, Hoover's, and other networks. Even when these pages are private (like a Facebook page), there are often invaluable clues left in plain sight (company affiliations, home towns, business relationships, links to blogs, etc.) that can help you tailor your offers to their needs. Other resources are Jigsaw and Pipl. You need to find the best ways to quickly research the types of clients you are getting.

If it's foreign investors, what do you need to know to proceed with follow-up? Identify your information needs and the fastest way to get it.

3. **Reach out in unique ways.** Businesspeople may filter you out of email because, in addition to all the spam and generic marketing, the normal volume of emails from associates and colleagues is already overwhelming. But people get very few direct messages through social media, and the messages they do get are usually from more trusted sources. If you can find a web prospect's social media page on LinkedIn, Facebook, or Twitter, experiment with sending him/her a direct message on that channel. Ben Kinney's team got a 67 percent increase in responses when they reached out to leads he had captured on his website via their social media profiles.

4. **Convert right from the start.** If you're ready to take it to the next level, ask people to sign up for appointments online to receive advanced offers. Always be making an offer. For instance, certain types of assessments or analyses, offers of customized deal lists, etc. Explain on your website that these services require a brief meeting to discuss the person's requirements. If they are serious about their needs, they'll be interested enough to sign up. However, you will have to be prepared to deliver what you offer, so train your junior staff to handle basic information-gathering meetings or to work with partners to deliver free services if you begin to get overwhelmed.

5. **Give them an out.** Always include an "opt out" option on your email campaigns, newsletters, or other types of communication, so

prospects can remove themselves from your list. Besides being the right thing to do, it also serves as a form of accountability. If you start to notice a large volume of prospects opting out of your newsletter or drip campaign, they've given you the gift of letting you know your current message isn't working. It's time to rework the program.

6. **Track, track, track.** Track every detail of your capture and conversion efforts. Whether you use reporting tools like Google Analytics or simply keep track in Excel, find the trends and leverage them. What offers are people responding to? What offers generate the most converted leads? How are people finding you online? Which ads were the most productive? If you don't know the answers to these questions, everything you do is a shot in the dark rather than part of a concerted strategy. You won't know where you should be investing more of your time and resources if you don't know what activities lead to conversion.

While the Internet gives you fabulously affordable methods for lead generation, it is *not* free. If you think of it that way, refusing to commit the resources necessary to make the investment of time and effort worthwhile, your returns will be limited. Yes, your resources are more constricted now than ever, so you must be strategic and focused. And remember, you'll need to spend as much time and effort crafting the message/delivery of your brand online as you have in all of your offline efforts. Consider the number of potential viewers of your website before you try to take the easiest or cheapest path. What you should be focused on is developing your expertise, sharing your knowledge, and helping people.

Many balk at adopting the approaches outlined in this tactic because they feel it will simply ask too much of them. It can seem like too much change for one person to manage at once, and all the brokers we spoke to felt that way when the Internet revolution first knocked on their door. What they discovered is that you don't have to change your business model: If your business is reliant on referrals, then simply leverage the tactics described here to augment your existing efforts. If your brokerage is reliant on new leads and new contacts, then employ the Internet and social media toward those efforts. Most often, your Internet lead generation strategy will mirror your offline business practices. And yes, you'll have to learn a few new tricks, but those tricks will let you do more with less and more business more efficiently.

TACTIC #7
PRICE TIGHT TO THE MARKET –
SHIFT PRICING STRATEGIES

Bad news isn't wine. It doesn't improve with age.

COLIN POWELL

Do primitive instincts impact a seller's ability to realistically price a property? Studies say yes. For all of our development over the millennia, there is a part of our thought processes driven by our instincts to survive. And to survive, your attention must be finely attuned to the negative risks inherent in a situation. That instinct leads to a tendency to focus more heavily on the threat of losing rather than opportunities for winning. Recent studies have shown how this behavior plays out in different aspects of life, even with hypothetical wins and losses associated with a coin toss. In an interview on NPR's *All Things Considered*, Eric Johnson, from Columbia Business School, explained that most people will take the bet, "If it's heads, you win $6, tails, you lose $1." But very few people will take the bet, "If it's heads, you win $6; tails, you lose $4"—even though, mathematically, if you took this bet over and over, you would walk away a winner. Odds are that you'll get heads as often as tails, you'll win as often as you lose, and your gains will outpace your losses. But our brains don't process it that way. We just know that "losing feels worse than winning feels good," according to NPR correspondent David Kestenbaum.

Recently Chris Mayer, professor of real estate at Columbia Business School, explored how this fear of loss affects property pricing in a shifted market. He would look at people who owned their condos outright and were selling them in a down market. Those who purchased their condos at the peak of the market would ask for a higher price and hold to it longer than those who purchased at a less-than-peak price. Selling for anything less than what they perceived the value to be felt like a loss, and in the sellers' minds, that loss outweighed the win of actually selling the condo.

When offering a broker opinion of value to a prospective client, it is crucial to use conservative and realistic pricing for today's market. Having a stable of overpriced, unsellable listings is a disservice to everyone involved. It is our fiduciary duty as trusted advisers to counsel our clients on the realities of what the market is "saying." One way we do this is by our monthly reporting to clients of what is happening with their property, our local market, and the regional and national markets.

Ken Wimberly,
Dallas, Texas

Figure 22 shows the severe drop in the commercial property price index from 2007 through mid-2011. Lease rates are also at a historical low, so brokers are left to play the role of economic psychologist with clients, helping them to focus on wins rather than losses by asking questions like, "What's more important to you: Immediate cash flow or return on investment? Better occupancy rates or better lease terms?" Most landlords and sellers will struggle to adjust their sense of value to the realities of the market, and some may be incapable of letting go of their fear of loss, pricing their properties out of the market. In those cases, there is little a broker can do.

When it comes to pricing, you must often present your client with a tough choice, and when you do, they'll look to you for assurances that you can't give. In the real world, few things are black and white. They want

COMMERCIAL PROPERTY PRICE INDEX

2001 Through Mid-2010

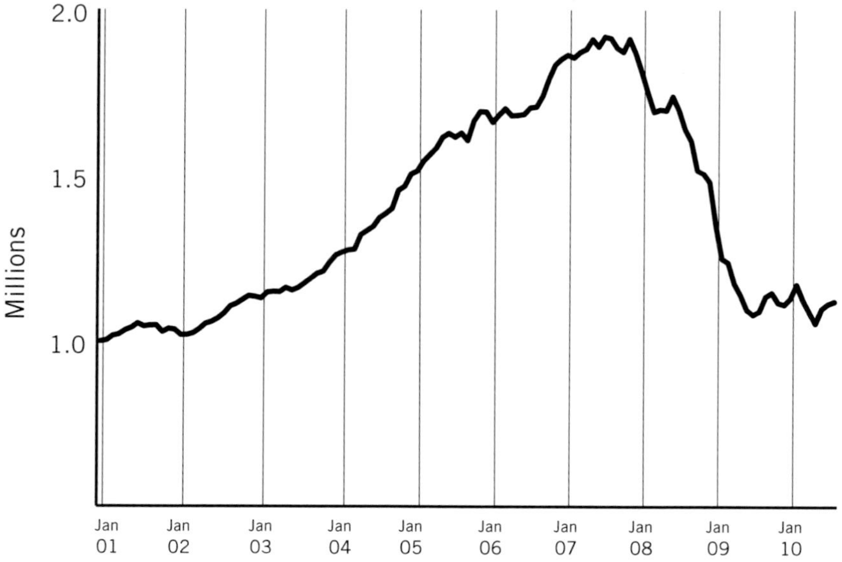

Figure 22: Moodys/REAL Commercial Property Price Index (CPPI)
(Source: MIT)

to hear you say, "If you price it at X, you'll have an offer in thirty days." *Then I'll know the sacrifice of value, income, or financial position is worth it*, they think. But in a shifted market, there are no guarantees. So what's a broker to do?

Remember, your clients need you to be the expert, to guide them through difficult decisions. It is your responsibility to help your clients price the property as tight to the market as possible, based on your market knowledge, network of experts, and research. You have to weigh what you know about the market with your understanding of your clients' problems and needs. You need to explore these critical questions:

1. Why is the client selling or leasing? What are their expectations—realistic or otherwise—and motivations?

2. How can I set realistic expectations and get the client focused on the "wins" of completing a transaction?

3. What is a tight-to-market price range for the property or space?

4. How can we make the property as attractive as possible or overcome hurdles for potential investors or tenants?

In a shifted market, your goal is to use this information to find the pricing point where your client can accept and minimize any losses and make the most of any wins.

KNOW YOUR CLIENT'S NEEDS AND MOTIVATIONS

Recall the statement from Tactic #5: You are in the business of solving your client's problems. Ultimately, your client must be satisfied with the final transaction. So the question of price must begin with a clear understanding of your client's problems and needs. Throughout the conversion process, particularly in the two meetings, you should have discovered those details. However, you may find that a client will be even more revealing with the specifics of their financials or proprietary business information after you have signed an agreement.

While the client may demand a pricing strategy that is not ideal for your brokerage cash flow (because it may take longer to close a transaction), you always have to prioritize the needs of the client. If you pressure them to make a decision they feel isn't aligned with their goals, you risk losing their trust. However, if they insist on pricing it at the high end of the range the market can support, initially, you will have to accept the price or decline the listing. If you take the listing, you can set expectations for revisiting the price point at a predetermined time or under predetermined conditions. For instance, if there is no interest in the property at the current pricing level after a set period of time, this becomes a trigger to have a reality-check conversation with the client. Sometimes clients will have a firmer grasp on the potential for their property than would ever be revealed in the comps and they will get their asking price. More often, the market will quickly inform them (with its silence) that they've overreached. And that's your opportunity to reprice the listing and get it in line with the reality of the marketplace.

> *Don't waste your time with listings that are overpriced. This leads to a waste of your time, and you are setting yourself and your client up for a lot of heartache and frustration. Sometimes it is better to let someone else take the listing at an inflated number and then be the second or third agent to get the listing after the landlord/seller has learned their lesson.*
>
> David Neault,
> Norco, California

Seller motivations. For your seller clients, dig deeper into the motivation for selling in a shifted market to develop a pricing strategy that satisfies their needs. Answer the questions shown in figure 23.

If the client is underwater and the property is distressed, you have to be clear about that from the start, ask for permission to involve the bank

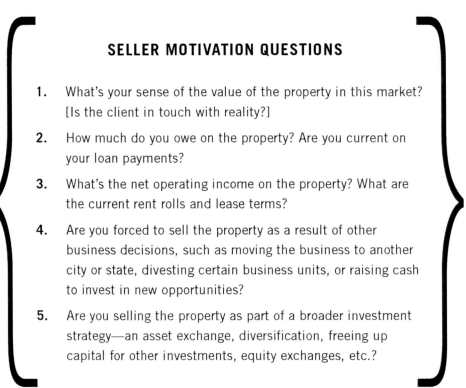

SELLER MOTIVATION QUESTIONS

1. What's your sense of the value of the property in this market? [Is the client in touch with reality?]

2. How much do you owe on the property? Are you current on your loan payments?

3. What's the net operating income on the property? What are the current rent rolls and lease terms?

4. Are you forced to sell the property as a result of other business decisions, such as moving the business to another city or state, divesting certain business units, or raising cash to invest in new opportunities?

5. Are you selling the property as part of a broader investment strategy—an asset exchange, diversification, freeing up capital for other investments, equity exchanges, etc.?

Figure 23

or noteholder, determine if a short sale is acceptable, and then develop a pricing strategy that will get the property sold at a price that the bank will accept. Or is there an opportunity to restructure the note? Recall the Chris Sands story from Tactic #4, and refer to Tactic #11 for more information on working with banks on distressed assets.

Although rare, there are clients who are in a strong financial position with their properties because they bought in a down market and can sell in the current market while still achieving strong ROI. If the client is moving their business from one state to another and has the capital to buy a new building without selling the current property, they may want to set a price that's on the high end of the market to test the waters and possibly extract a greater return. If this is the case, you must set the expectation that, if activity or showings for the property are minimal in the first few months, you may need to reassess the price. If the client is trying to free up capital to invest in an available property with a greater potential ROI, maximizing the sales price on the current property may be less important than getting access to capital as quickly as possible.

Landlord motivations. While sellers are still present in a shifted market, transaction velocity and volume will decline, and thus you will find more landlord/tenant leasing clients (see Tactic #11), Markets of the Moment). For landlords with space for lease, the leasing needs seem fairly straightforward, right? Improve occupancy, attract the best tenants, get the highest rates possible. However, any one of these points may need to be top priority, so you'll have to probe for clues, starting with the questions in figure 24.

LANDLORD MOTIVATION QUESTIONS

1. What are your lease rate expectations?
2. What is the current occupancy rate for the property?
3. What do the rent rolls look like—current lowest and highest lease rates, lease expiration outlook, etc.?
4. How has net operating income changed on the property in the past six to twelve months?

Figure 24

If a client has a 50 percent vacancy rate, they may care little about negotiating for higher lease rates and more about getting new tenants paying rent as soon as possible to generate greater cash flow. If the majority of the current tenants are paying above-market rates on older leases that won't expire for some time, the client may be willing to offer lower rates for new tenants. Ultimately, the client will want to maintain or improve net operating income, so understanding the cost basis and debt on the property will be critical in developing a strategy that meets the client's needs.

That said, it is still your responsibility to establish realistic expectations and to get the client focused on the possibilities rather than what they're losing.

CREATE A POSITIVE PRICING MINDSET

We all know that a shifted market is a buyers' market, so sellers and landlords often walk into and out of shift-time transactions with a sour taste in their mouths. And you may too, as you earn smaller and smaller commission checks on deals that would have garnered 50 percent more income three years ago. But you have to combat the malaise you and your client may feel as prices drop if you want to get deals done. You have to reveal the risks of overpricing if they want to get to a closed transaction, but you also have to present the opportunities available to them to help them get over the emotional and intellectual hurdle of the loss they are likely facing in the short term.

The seller mindset. For sellers with positive equity, the key is to get them focused on the possibilities of better returns on the capital they reallocate to alternative investments. If they're being forced to sell for some other reason and have elevated pricing expectations, you'll need to help them develop this mindset. You can start by sharing some statistics on the reduction in commercial transactions. For instance, in 2011, commercial transactions were down close to 75 percent compared to 2007 levels, primarily because of the disconnect between what sellers were asking and buyers were offering.

Next, ask the question, "Do you want to sell it today and take a loss, or do you want to hold it and wait possibly a few years to earn the return you're hoping for?" Using a break-even model can help even the most recalcitrant clients understand the logic of earning a better return faster by investing the capital elsewhere. "You've got a $10 million property that's down 40 percent to $6 million (and we know that's likely in the current shifted market based on the CPPI graph at the beginning of the chapter). If we assume a 4 percent return over the coming years (and even that may be optimistic), it will take you about thirteen years to get back to your original equity investment. If you took that $6 million and invested in a distressed property where you could potentially earn a 10 percent annual return, you can be back at $10 million in less than six years."

Instead of focusing on the $4 million loss, you want them focused on the opportunities they can take advantage of with their $6 million equity in a buyers' market of a lifetime. It's just a matter of reallocating assets, because a poor investment is a poor investment, especially in a shifted market. Cut the losses and find an opportunity for better long-term prospects and a better return on investment.

For clients with negative equity or who can no longer afford the property because of reduced cash flow or operating income, the goal is to get them out as quickly as possible and minimize any additional losses. Some of these people may even have personal guarantees on the property that they need to get out from under. Get them focused on protecting their financial status (by avoiding bankruptcy or foreclosure, for instance) and moving on. For short sales, it's all about finding an offer the bank will accept.

The landlord mindset. Generally speaking, landlords in a shifted market should not be focused on return *on* investment, but on return *of* investment. You have to shift their focus from returns and toward survival, and that means cash flow. Empty buildings have zero cash flow and offer negative returns. While improving occupancy at low lease rates may not improve ROI, it will certainly improve cash flow.

Focus on the importance of attracting quality tenants—stable businesses with good credit—with short leases (three to five years) and, yes, low rental rates. Once you get tenants into the building, the relationship becomes sticky—they are apt not to move. In a few years, the landlord can increase the rent to reflect normalized market rates. If the landlord is professional and provides strong customer service, they won't likely lose the tenant.

If the building is vacant, you for sure are going to lose money. However, if you can take this tenant for an amount that will at least allow you to break even, then in three years time we can reevaluate.

Peter Pessetto,
Raleigh, North Carolina

Of course, this strategy will be in direct opposition to what tenants will be trying to achieve—longer leases locked in at lower rates—so negotiations may be fierce in a shifted market. We'll talk more about the issues of representing tenants in Tactic #9 Create Urgency.

Obviously, an ideal client is a landlord who owns a building outright or who has owned the building for a long time. Because their cost basis is so low, they can focus on cash flow, which gives them a huge advantage over their competition on lease rates. For the vast majority of your landlord clients, it will be better to have a tenant at a lower rental rate than vacant space. Robert Tufts from New Orleans, Louisiana, fully understands this concept with his investment portfolio. "We constantly attempt to be ahead of the market from a lease rate and concession perspective with quality tenants. Most landlords are reactionary to rates and concessions and thus lose the quality transactions to the proactive and creative landlords like myself."

While understanding the client's motivations and establishing a positive perspective are crucial to making transactions happen, ultimately, your recommendations must be based on your knowledge of what the market can support.

ESTABLISH TIGHT-TO-MARKET PRICES

Shifted markets can change month to month. If you are not digging to find real, current market rates, sales, and leasing trends for your clients, you are failing them. Without the most current information, your approach and your sense of pricing will lag behind the market and you will find it difficult to get deals done.

Pricing to sell. In a shifted real estate market, lease rates, vacancy rates, and investor expectations magnify each other to produce a triple hit on valuations. Establishing a price that is tight to the market requires brokers to leverage their expertise, market knowledge, and networks. But if they price a property well for its perceived market value, they may actually get multiple offers on the property, creating a bidding war that raises the price above the asking. Figure 25 presents the key tactics for pricing to move sales properties.

TACTICS FOR SETTING SALE PRICES TIGHT TO THE MARKET

1. Weight older comparable sales lowest.

2. Weight income highest, but base it on conservative projections of future net operating income.

3. Use discounted replacement value, particularly for distressed properties.

4. For distressed properties, consult with the bank early to determine an acceptable short sale price.

Figure 25

Comparable sales in a shifted market can be very challenging, because little is selling and older sales are simply irrelevant. Your best bet is to focus your research on properties that have sold in the last six months. And if the market is still shifting, sales in the last six months may be irrelevant three months from now, when you are still trying to find a buyer. Even then, the *real sales price* may be hidden behind concessions and any number of contractual agreements that aren't available to the general public. Get plugged in and use your network to discover real sales prices. What a property is listed for and what it actually sells for could be vastly different. In markets with a commercial MLS, there will be more visibility on actual sales prices. Become an expert with your taxing authority and the systems they use to record property information and valuations. Turn to your network of mortgage and title companies, pore over public records, and ask the other brokers or appraisers in your network. You aren't asking them to reveal confidential information, but they can help you establish a range that might be appropriate based on the transactions they've closed. If you're going into a market where there are no sales at all, be cautious because the lender's appraisal might come in lower than your price and jeopardize the funding.

In a shifted market, historic and even current net operating income is irrelevant in valuations. Instead buyers are valuing office and retail properties based upon conservative estimates for future rental rates and future NOI. As leases expire, they will likely renew at lower rates, so buyers anticipate discounted NOI and cash flows. That said, income is likely the most accurate determinant of value and should be reviewed carefully, even for user-owner properties or SBA properties (which we'll discuss in Tactic #10).

Cash buyers are often most interested in replacement cost in a shifted market. For distressed assets; for which other forms of valuation are so uncertain, particularly those with substantial vacancies; buyers may want a fairly steep discount to replacement cost. This helps them take into account the cost of refurbishing the property. Phoenix broker Brock Danielson reports that in the slump of 2008 to 2010, multifamily properties simply could not be priced based on income approach: "Instead, we have to use a 'price per pound' strategy based on direct replacement cost. For example, a multifamily development may cost $255 per square foot to build, but it is currently being sold for $100 per square foot. Now, it still may not have a good cap rate, but it is a bargain if you were ever to consider building a similar property from scratch. Therefore, if a buyer believes that the market will recover and you can help them determine a way to make the property have a positive cash flow at the discounted price point, they can weather the storm and ride the valuation back up. In fact, you may find many properties that will sell on 50 percent discount of replacement cost. This indeed is a great time to buy."

For short sales on distressed assets, you have to bring the bank in from the beginning. Short sales can be difficult to navigate because they involve three parties: the owner, the bank, and the buyer. If you represent the owner, know that they aren't the final decision maker, the bank is; nothing will happen without the bank's agreement. That said, the bank would much rather be servicing the debt than owning the property. They don't want to assume the costs and responsibilities of ownership; it's not their business. So to understand pricing parameters for short sales, be sure to discuss ranges for offers the bank might consider early in the process and understand the existing debt ramifications on the transaction.

The hardest thing now is valuation. You become an economist first, a broker second. As we look in the crystal ball to the market's future, this is the cloudiest market we've ever had. This creates fear in buyers and sellers.

Brock Danielson,
Phoenix, Arizona

Pricing to lease. For your landlord clients, understanding pricing trends and staying ahead of them is a key differentiator for your practice. It is much more difficult to uncover true lease rates than it is to research actual sales prices. Many landlords are basing their expectations on face rates: what properties are advertised for, what they've heard about current lease rates in competing buildings, what the uninformed market believes about current lease rates. Oftentimes, the actual rate is a discounted one that takes into account the cost of all concessions made in the lease negotiations—free rent for periods of time; tenant improvement dollars; move dollars; furniture, fixtures, and equipment (FF&E); and other concessions that effectively lower the actual rental income being earned. For instance, the face rate may be $20 per square foot for a five-year lease, but if the landlord has offered one year of free rent, this would equate to an actual rate of $16 per square foot. Landlords try to hide the actual rates and concessions, because they don't want their existing tenants and others to expect the same deals.

The difference between actual rates and face rates can be vast, and your ability to educate your client on actual rates is the most powerful expertise you can offer. But how do you discover actual rates? Figure 26 presents the top three tactics.

TACTICS FOR SETTING LEASE RATES TIGHT TO THE MARKET

1. Identify real comparables, based on an expanded audience of prospective tenants.

2. Use your network to uncover actual rates.

3. Start slightly below market, but prepare your client for additional concessions and even lower rates.

Figure 26

First, identify real lease comparables. Tour competing properties to get a sense of what is being offered. Use all of your knowledge of the market you've gained through your prospecting efforts to clarify who the competition is. But also be aware that, in a shift, many tenants will be looking to upgrade to a higher-tier building (from C to B or from B to A), because a better building is now within their financial reach. So as you consider comparables, consider that if you have a B property, you aren't just competing with other B properties for B tenants—you're also now competing with A properties. You'll need to take that into account in your pricing strategy if you don't want high vacancies.

Second, use your network to uncover actual rates. In any market, there's a top tier of brokers who know the rates in the current market. If you are a landlord representative, you may be working with an array of tenant representatives who all have information on recently closed transactions: the rent stated in the agreement and all of the concessions granted. Sometimes they share knowledge with you as a part of their negotiations. "We're getting free rent and a lower lease rate offered at another property, but we prefer this property, so if you can go lower, the client will likely go with your property." This is helpful, but passive.

The best way to discover actual rates is to be active in the market-place; for example, when you have two or three active requirements for space with quality tenants, all the surrounding landlords will be offering the best deals and most concessions possible in an attempt to bring your client to their building. Again, success begets success, as well as providing you with excellent market information.

To be proactive, query your network of tenant reps and others who might have insight. They won't reveal confidential information, but they will identify current concessions being made in the market, ranges of lease rates they are currently seeing, and so on. If you ask for information, you need to be prepared to share information. You can't horde market knowledge and expect others to not do the same. I'm talking about cooperation here, not collusion, because you wouldn't be sharing this type of information with your competitors.

And if you have diversified sufficiently, you may be playing both a tenant representative and landlord representative role with different clients. This situation offers you unique insights that you can leverage to help all of your clients without revealing confidential information or creating conflicts of interest.

Finally, set lease rates tight to the actual market rates, but prepare your client for additional concessions and even lower rates if quality tenants demand it. Of course you will try to get market rates because it is in the best interest of your client, but be honest about the actual rates and explain that they may need to accept a lower one if an offer comes in from a high-credit tenant. When appropriate, pricing slightly below market sends a signal to all tenants that you are in a deal-making mode and thus will attract more tours and ultimately more offers.

Peter Pessetto of Raleigh-Durham, North Carolina, had a landlord who was a real estate attorney, so he was knowledgeable and experienced. But that still didn't solve the pricing problem. "His office condo property was in a good location and in good condition. By rights, it should have been valued at $14 or $15 per square foot, but it had been vacant for eight months. We put it back out there for $12.50 and got a tenant in right away, with a solid three-year lease and no extension clauses. If he had not understood or had not wanted to lower the price, I would have walked away."

If your client isn't prepared to make transactions based on actual rates rather than market face rates, you will likely sit on a vacant building.

BREAK DOWN BUYER AND TENANT HURDLES

In Tactics #8, #9, and #10, we'll discuss how to make transactions happen by staging, overcoming objections, and identifying creative financing options. But in any pricing negotiation, you can work with your clients to leverage unique approaches to overcoming hurdles and closing transactions at a price or rate that's more satisfactory.

Buyer hurdles. In a shifted market, buyers are concerned about future NOI, particularly on lease-based properties. Sellers can leverage master leasing and staggered lease expirations to combat those fears and set a higher sales price on a property.

If you have a client who really needs to get $8 million for a property that would likely sell for $6 million in the current market, particularly because of a higher-than-ideal vacancy rate, you might encourage the individual to propose a master lease. Your client would agree to pay the new owner rental payments for any unleased space for a period of time. This can be an appealing arrangement for both sides if the vacancy rate is high and if the buyers are particularly interested in acquiring the property for current income.

Additionally, you might also have to stagger rent roles to improve the future picture of NOI and cash flow. If the property has a number of tenants with lease expirations at the same time, buyers will be wary. No investor wants a multitenant property with a large portion of the leases expiring in the same year. They know that leases will have to be renegotiated at potentially lower rates or they may lose the tenants altogether. Approach the tenants and negotiate extensions on the current leases for different lengths of time, so that the risk over any given time frame is lessened.

You have to be cautious with this approach, though, because it will be equally unappealing to potential buyers to be locked into low-performing leases with poor tenants. Be strategic and only extend leases with the quality tenants at reasonable rates. Your experience pays off here: You will know where the thresholds are and how to find the balance between a staggered full occupancy and rental rates.

Tenant hurdles. Keep in mind that a quality building owner will pay up for a quality tenant, one way or another—if not through a reduced lease rate, then in concessions to help overcome the prospective tenant's hurdles. You have to work with your landlords to uncover the obstacles that are keeping a quality tenant out of your building, and then find ways to overcome those objections. You have to be proactive and creative in a shifted market.

When you are representing a seller and there is a potential buyer interested, have the seller extend an offer to the buyer. While somewhat untraditional, more often than not the buyer will counter. Regardless of the counteroffer, you have now brought the buyer into negotiations. Many deals have gotten done by merely bringing otherwise unlikely parties together.

Matthew Rasche,
Chicago, Illinois

Some approaches you might consider are buying out existing leases, taking over a current lease and then subletting the space, funding moving costs, funding build-outs, and offering options on additional space or on smaller spaces in case space requirements change. This last one can be particularly appealing in a shifting economy when companies anticipate reducing headcount and thus need less space.

As you work with building owners, counsel them to be much more vigilant about staying connected to what is going on with their tenants' businesses and to be as flexible and accommodating with their current tenants' needs as possible. It is often wise to rework a lease with a current tenant rather than lose them or force them out of business.

Anything you can do to reduce tenants' costs is a leverage point. For instance, when making repairs or upgrades, look to go green to improve energy efficiency and reduce tenants' expenses. And the more landlords can negotiate with vendors to reduce the costs of operating the building, the greater the savings they'll be able to pass on to tenants.

Every transaction in a shifted market—lease or sale—will involve protracted negotiations, and the more you can leverage the negotiation process to solve investor and tenant problems, the more successful you will be at closing the transaction and reaching an agreement that satisfies all parties.

FINAL LESSONS FOR BROKERS FROM A SHIFTED MARKET

In a shifted market, there are a lot of properties and yet only a few for sale at realistic prices. The lessons for brokers are often discovered after much wasted time, effort, and resources. And brokers often overlook the lessons they should learn about their own practices. So let me share three critical lessons with you:

1. **Don't be afraid to ask for marketing fees up front**. If you are concerned that, after considerable discussion and research, the seller is not prepared to price the property to sell, you should either advise the seller to hold the property and wait for an improvement in the marketplace or you should ask for a draw against future commissions for expenses. Marketing and listing a commercial property can be very expensive and time consuming, taxing resources you don't have to waste. Or you can take Jeremy Cyrier's approach outlined in Tactic #5 and get paid for your creative, prospect-focused marketing efforts up front on all your listings.

2. **Be flexible with commissions.** As your clients negotiate prices, your commission is one additional financial burden they have to account for. Larry Culbertson of Atlanta, Georgia, has a creative method for assisting exclusive clients who may be facing unexpected costs associated with a transaction, such as build-out or master leases. "The solution that we offer is a quarterly commission payout structure," he explains. "Rather than asking for the entire commission up front, we are allowing the owner to pay commissions as they receive rents. I have a little risk in the game, but I am building a long-term relationship with the landlord and the tenant (who got a better rate). I receive my procurement fee at lease signing and establish the quarterly payments in an agreement to include potential late fees. In this way, we can make a win/win/win situation for the owner, the tenant, and our firm. This practice has given me a competitive edge."

3. **The first offer is often the best, even if it's discounted.** This is a lesson for brokers and their clients. Reagan Dixon put a major downtown office building on the market at the beginning of a downturn and priced it at $135 million. "After time, we received an offer for $109 million. It was a credible offer, but lower than the asking price. We also received an offer for $135 million from an investor who had not even seen the property. After their due diligence, they changed their offer to only $95 million. Of course, by then, the first offer was gone. The property eventually sold a year later for $79 million." Timing, and realistic pricing expectations, is everything.

Pricing in a shifted market is rarely fun. No matter how well you've qualified or prepared your clients, you'll see a look of disappointment on their faces when you present them with the reality of the market. But have confidence that you are delivering the hard truth they need—that valuable decisive leadership—that will get them to a closed transaction, freed-up capital, or improved occupancy. And that is why they hired you to begin with.

TACTIC #8
STAND OUT FROM THE COMPETITION –
PROPERTY STAGING STRATEGIES

Vision is the art of seeing the invisible.
JONATHAN SWIFT

In 2009, in the beginning of a shifted market, business startups were at a fourteen-year high according to the Kauffman Index of Entrepreneurial Activity. It turns out that new businesses have launched in very steady numbers every year for the past thirty years, recession or not. Businesses that start during a recession may have a better survival rate than ones that start during stronger economies. Why? Because they usually have little access to capital and so must be smart and strategic about finding money and using it. Forced frugality, careful planning, and clear strategies for growth in a tough economy create strong companies that can stand the test of time.

Of course, if you represent a landlord, this is good news: As startups start up and grow, they need office space. What is their biggest need? *Flexibility*. And they aren't alone. In times of uncertainty, everybody is looking for a hedge against the unforeseen or an edge against the competition, so showcasing the flexibility—opportunities to fulfill a variety of needs—of any space for lease or sale is a key tactic for distinguishing your property in a shifted market. The added bonus of flexibility is that the property will appeal to a wider range of tenants and investors.

While staging, as a term and practice, is more common in the residential industry, it is equally important in commercial. It just means something a bit different: More than just ensuring a property is clean and in good condition, commercial staging entails all of the things we do to ensure that a property is as appealing as possible to as many buyers or tenants as possible.

And that is never more important than in a shifted market, when precious few are looking to actually buy or lease, and those that are will be looking for high-value properties and have a vast array of options. In times like these, "standing out from the competition" becomes a critical tactic for both you and your clients. The first impression will be the only impression; buyers or tenants who don't think the space meets their needs—now or in the future—won't bother coming back a second time to ask questions. They have other properties vying for their attention, and they know that somebody will get it right from the start.

The most successful commercial investors are often those who can spot profit potential in properties that others overlook. They can detect "hidden value" in cosmetic and structural improvements, in rezoning, in new tenants, in alternative uses for the property. and even advantageous demographic trends others wouldn't think to look for. Your ability as a commercial real estate broker to do the same is a key reason your clients hire you to represent their properties. When staging, your mission is to spotlight opportunity starkly and highlight competitive advantages in such detail that the most myopic buyers and tenants will recognize the value from a mile away!

Here are four ways to successfully stage properties in a shifted market:

1. Convert properties to expand the market.

2. Stage properties to highlight flexibility.

3. Increase awareness of opportunities—onsite and online.

4. Educate prospects to build clarity and confidence.

1. CONVERT PROPERTIES TO EXPAND THE MARKET

A key strategy for doing this in a shifted market is conversion. It often requires little investment on the part of the landlord or owner and can dramatically improve the chances of closing transactions with tenants or investors.

A prime example is condominiums. In a hot market, it's common for owners of multifamily developments to do some upgrades and convert their properties into condos to take advantage of the broader market of home buyers. In a shifted market, the reverse happens. It's not uncommon to see a new condominium built at the top of the market struggling with less than 50 percent of the units sold. As bubbles burst, the chances of selling those units become slim. What should the owners do? The answer is to convert the property to multifamily. Most condo contracts allow for the conversion under certain circumstances, so owners are usually within their rights to do so—especially when the owner controls more than 50 percent of the complex units. More people lease than buy in a shifted market, and multifamily properties are a market of the moment that we'll discuss in more detail in Tactic #11. This simple conversion, while it might not make current unit owners happy, can dramatically increase occupancy and cash flow. And if the property is for sale, it would be far more appealing to investors as multifamily when it is fully leased. This same technique can sometimes apply in the conversion of condos to hotel properties. Again, in a shift, it is easier to get nightly "rentals" than the sale of a unit.

Additionally, conversion principles apply to other types of properties for sale or lease in a shifted market. For instance, retail properties can expand their tenant prospect base by converting space to office use. Attracting businesses that find foot traffic and greater visibility with the general public appealing—insurance offices, real estate offices, banking offices, and others—will improve occupancy levels.

But conversion can be particularly important for "B"- and "C"-level office buildings, which are hard hit in a shifted market. Tenants in B and C buildings are often small businesses or businesses that may be financially unstable. In a tough economy, many may go under. And those tenants who are stronger financially have vast opportunities to upgrade their space with a minimal increase in rent. When leases at "A" buildings become more affordable, tenants who can afford to will move on from their B- or C-level facilities. The result: skyrocketing vacancies. So what should a commercial broker do when representing these buildings?

First, counsel the landlord to consider converting some or all of the space to quasi-industrial for flex tenants—those who need office space and warehouse or manufacturing space under one roof. With a bit of demolition to open up useful space in the back of the building and the installation of a rolling or sectional door, the space would be more appealing to the types of tenants it's likely to attract in a shift. Barry Bounds, managing director in Denver, Colorado, secured a new listing with this tactic. "There was an older class B-C single-story office park located in Denver that was struggling with a high vacancy rate. We approached the owner with a conversion strategy to flex space because the market vacancy rate was much lower. We obtained the listing and reduced the vacancy rate from 40 percent to less than 10 percent. "Second, if it is a property for sale, highlight opportunities for conversion that might be supported by government programs. For instance, conversion to a "green building" with energy-efficient upgrades that could be financed with government funds could be an option as well. This might be a good approach if the property is located in a highly visible and desirable location.

Finally—and this is a conversion tactic for *all* office, retail, and industrial buildings with low occupancy that are for sale—consider converting the investment property to a potential SBA property. The Small Business Administration of the federal government offers loans that a business can use to purchase its facilities. The only caveat is that the business must occupy at least 51 percent of the space for the property to qualify. If your building is at 50 or 60 percent

Putting a "for lease" sign in a building that you really want to sell is a good idea; you might be able to convert a prospecting lease customer to an SBA buyer.

Nancy Lemas,
Boise, Idaho

occupancy and you have little hope of getting tenants in to improve the appeal of the property to investors, advise the owner to consider buying out or canceling the leases of the less financially stable tenants. If you can reduce the occupancy rate below 49 percent, the property would be eligible for an SBA buyer. You might be reducing its appeal to general investors, but its appeal wasn't strong to begin with. Ideally, you might convince some tenants to move to a month-to-month lease that would give them flexibility and would give you the opportunity to end the lease quickly if you found a potential SBA buyer.

Even if a landlord or owner chooses not to convert a space before trying to lease or sell it, revealing to prospective buyers and tenants that they are willing to cover conversion costs can go a long way toward meeting those individuals' needs, and closing more transactions.

2. STAGE PROPERTIES TO HIGHLIGHT FLEXIBILITY

The best commercial brokers stage their properties to ensure the features are competitively highlighted and to improve perceived value. In this sense, we're taking about the traditional meaning of staging where you're improving and showcasing a property's condition and amenities. The goal is to maximize the perceived value, because while pricing attracts showings, *perceived value attracts offers*. Recall from Tactic #5 Jeremy Cyrier, and how he developed perceived value by renaming the property "Technology Innovation Place." And perceived value is influenced by how effectively the property meets prospects' expectations and needs—flexibility being at the top of the list for many buyers and tenants in a shifted market. Price and perceived value are inseparable. When the asking price seems lower than the perceived value warrants, they see an opportunity and worry that it won't last on the market. And that concern converts to offers on your listing.

When Dan Henderson of Charleston, South Carolina, saw the old storage warehouse that a bank asked him to market, he knew immediately that some work was necessary. "When we first went in, the electricity was off, so we had no idea what we had. When we got the lights turned on, we saw that it was so full of junk and trash you couldn't even walk through it. What kind of buyer would have been interested in that building in its current condition? If we had tried to sell it while it still looked like hell, the buyer would have gone in and said, 'Hey, this is going to be a steal!' We would have ended up selling it for pennies on the dollar. Instead, we cleaned it out and put on a fresh coat of paint. In the end, we're investing $10,000 to $15,000 to spruce it up. Now it looks like an investment property—a respectable, clean, and ready-to-use space. The owner originally hoped to get $200,000. Now we can expect to sell it for $350,000."

If you're keeping score at home, Dan's investment in basic staging may earn as much as a fifteen fold return. While not every improvement will offer that yield, investments in condition tend to generate the highest returns. But ensuring a property shows well may not be simple in a shifted market. Vacancies have increased and rents have plummeted in many markets. Beleaguered owners have been forced to dip into reserve accounts, or worse, make a cash call to their investor group. As a result, many have eliminated every expense possible, including routine maintenance and upkeep. So your first job is to conduct a thorough property evaluation and soberly analyze it from a buyer or tenant's perspective.

Particularly when dealing with vacant or short sale properties, make sure the power is on so that prospects can actually see the property's potential. Make sure that basic landscaping has been maintained, old signage has been removed, old carpeting has been ripped out, and concrete floors have been power washed. A fresh coat of paint inside or out may be warranted. If the building HVAC systems, roof, or foundation are not in good repair, you'll have to conduct a cost-benefit analysis to determine whether the owner should invest in major repairs.

The level of staging beyond the basics depends on the nature of the property and the nature of the potential. If you can expand the market by better highlighting how the space can meet a variety of tenant needs, then it's probably worth the investment. Before you consider how best to improve a property's perceived value, do your due diligence. Get to know your market and competition better than any other broker. Research and tour other buildings—know every sizable space available, the pros and cons of each, and how your property can favorably compete.

If you are marketing a lease property, remember that many tenants are looking to upgrade in a shifted market. If you have an A building, you want to make it appealing to A clients, but also to B clients who are looking to upgrade the quality of their space. If you have a B property, open it up to B- and C-level tenants. Query different types of tenants about their needs.

Use the trends you discover to highlight the opportunities of the spaces you represent. The best way to do this with office space is to build a spec suite. This type of suite, while it could involve a substantial investment that many landlords may be hesitant to make, offers multiple benefits. First, a lot of tenants need to be shown the potential of a space; they can't visualize it on their own. Second, for prospects who need to move quickly, you have a move-in-ready opportunity for them. If every space available in a building requires three to six months of build-out before tenants can move in, you're going to lose a lot of potential tenants.

Third, you can develop the spec suite in a way that offers maximum flexibility, ideal for smaller tenants, as incubator space for start-ups, or for businesses that believe they'll be expanding or contracting as the market continues to evolve. Build out a larger space, but let potential tenants know that you are willing to break it up into smaller units if they need less space. Or develop a few smaller units and let tenants know they can quickly be combined as they grow. You'll have to convince what may be a cash-strapped landlord to invest a bit of money, but a spec suite can help you capture more tenants.

Another great strategy for increasing both the perceived and real value for either buyers or tenants is to prenegotiate the transfer of furniture, fixtures, and equipment (FF&E) with tenants who are leaving. I have seen companies walk away from massive investments in FF&E for pennies on the dollar. Sometimes, a company wants to negotiate on FF&E because they are cash strapped, downsizing, or going under—all of these can be common in a shifted market. But amazingly, large corporations will walk away from millions of dollars in improvements and IT infrastructure because they are moving into a new space and want new furniture and equipment to go along with it. One international corporation I know of walked away from approximately $3 million in FF&E for about $300,000. And because the landlord got the FF&E for such a minimal cost, they could offer turnkey space to tenants for a price lower than the perceived value, making it highly attractive. Negotiating FF&E creates a turnkey solution for tenants at a time when they may need it the most (when they don't have their own funds to invest). And when selling a property, the return on investment on FF&E can be substantial.

While spec suites and FF&E are great techniques, it is your responsibility to ensure that the perceived value is as high as possible for as broad a range of prospects as possible, regardless of what the owner or landlord is willing to invest in the property. Only then will the property present to the widest range of prospective buyers and tenants.

3. INCREASE AWARENESS OF OPPORTUNITIES—ONSITE AND ONLINE

The hallmark of a shifted market is rapid changes in available properties—so rapid, it's hard for brokers who represent investors and tenants to keep up, and certainly difficult for the uninitiated investor or tenant to stay informed. Your goal is to improve awareness in the market of what you have to offer, to keep your property top of mind. The best way to do that is through open houses, prospect tours, and your website.

Face-to-face, onsite meetings—open houses for brokers and tours for prospects—allow you to highlight the best features of a property, to sell the "vision." That vision is at the heart of what differentiates you from the competition. Yet owners and brokers aren't the only ones who are concerned about cash outlays in a shifted market, and landlords who are working hard to keep marketing costs to a minimum often eliminate open houses. That is a misjudgment. Unless they see a property, investor and tenant representatives often don't understand its potential or how it fits with their clients' needs. Keep your investment in open houses tight, but absolutely do not stop doing them.

Both open houses and tours offer you an opportunity to broadcast points of flexibility based on what you learn about prospects' needs, either directly or from other brokers. You can do walk-throughs of conversions your clients are willing to consider and hint at concessions they're willing to make. If FF&E transferred from past tenants, you can show off turnkey spaces that are move-in ready.

When setting up tours specifically, consider the following recommendations:

1. Initially, meet to discuss the property at a nearby or onsite restaurant or coffee shop. People will be working in that location and will value local amenities.

2. If possible, set the appointment at peak traffic times for retail and multifamily and off-peak times for office or industrial prospects. Showing the buyer traffic counts on paper is good, but showing them visible traffic flow in person is better.

3. Reserve a good space for the prospect in the parking garage to create the impression of an easy commute and easy parking!

4. Make sure the building manager and engineer are aware that a prospect is coming, and have them greet the individual by name at the door. Every tenant wants to feel special, plus they may have questions about the facility that only the manager or engineer can address.

5. Arrange for a space planner to meet the prospect during a tour to offer creative ideas and visions for the space. For more interested prospects, offer to do a free space plan or test fit and arrange to chalk out where the walls, cubicles, or other tenant improvements would be located.

While you need to be proactive in your marketing efforts, your clients need to be proactively involved too. When the market is down, it's not uncommon for cash-strapped landlords to become unresponsive to tenant needs. What results is a general tenant malaise and prospects who survey properties with a bad taste in their mouths, expecting that the moment the contract is signed, their needs will move to the bottom of a landlord's priority list. Therefore, your landlord clients should be at your open houses and building managers and engineers should be present for tours. They can answer questions you may be unable to, they can be friendly and helpful, and they can prove to potential tenants that they are motivated to meet their needs, whatever those needs may be, and that they have a strong customer service ethic. Proactive landlord and property management involvement is a great way to impress prospects and differentiate your listings.

That said, when navigating competing schedules, the highest priority is to make seeing the property easy for prospects and their brokers. So if they only have a particular window open and there's no possible way for building representatives to be available, make getting the clients into the space the priority. And, in worst cases, if you need to put a lockbox on the building so that the prospect can stop in and see it between meetings or whenever they have a few spare moments in their busy schedule, just do it. You can follow up or tour the property with them another time.

As we discussed in Tactic #6, these days, potential investors and tenants may be scouring the Internet, searching for ideal properties. Consequently, the listings on your website are often your first

Making it easy to buy is something that many commercial brokers really need to learn from residential agents. Sometimes commercial real estate brokers are their own worst enemy: They make it so hard to see a building. If the building is vacant, I'll go buy a lockbox to put on it: that way I can direct a buyer to see the property at their convenience, and then show up or follow up.

Dan Henderson,
Charleston, South Carolina

opportunity to "show" a property. In today's shifting commercial market, Internet marketing is a *must* for virtually all of your commercial listings. The information you post must be comprehensive and must properly showcase the property to appeal to a variety of prospects. Recall Jeremy Cyrier's positioning approach to the information presented in online listings, which we discussed in Tactic #5. Keep that in mind in terms of how you market the property on your website. If you think you have information that makes the property appealing, don't hold back. In particular, try offering the following:

1. Create a foundational (rather than customized) marketing presentation that explains how the property will work to meet the specific needs of the target market, but be careful not to get too niche. Include multiple photographs and annotate the photos. Showing the vision to prospects is like telling a story, and the more specific and compelling you can make that story, the more likely the property will intrigue prospects.

2. Back up claims about the property with case studies and testimonials. If it's a leasing property, include stories from current tenants in the building to substantiate the property's benefits, as well as the level of service building management provides.

3. Put yourself in the shoes of your prospects for the property. What information is imperative to helping them make a good buy or lease decision? Present as much of that information on your website as you can, such as analysis of the demographics of the surrounding area, recent comparable sales, surrounding amenities, traffic information, or any relevant studies on the area or property. Site To Do Business is an excellent source for this critical information.

You have multiple opportunities to showcase your properties and highlight their value and potential—don't squander them. Put in the effort and resources to ensure the first impression is the best you can offer.

4. EDUCATE PROSPECTS TO BUILD CLARITY AND CONFIDENCE

As a commercial broker, you understand the thought processes and needs of a buyer or tenant. By focusing on their business needs rather than on a transaction, you have an opportunity to educate, to clarify the opportunity, and to build confidence that your property is the right property for them. All of the work that we discussed in Tactics #4 and #5 on building expertise, leading with knowledge, and freely sharing your expertise can be leveraged now. Your mission is to make every advantage the property offers as clear as possible to your prospects, to anticipate what buyers and tenants will want to know and when, and to make it easy to close the transaction.

A buyer or tenant needs to have confidence that their business will benefit from the terms and provisions of the purchase or lease. Ask questions, find out what prospects need, and be ready with precise information. Fear of making a bad decision because of uncertainty in the market or economy is often the highest hurdle that you have to help the buyer or tenant clear. For many, this fear can only be overcome with data. Even when the numbers aren't perfect, there is a feeling of confidence that is generated in the buyer or tenant by just knowing that they have the information in hand.

Companies like eBay, Amazon.com, and Apple spend hundreds of millions each year perfecting the user experience. They pour over usability studies and obsessively measure click-throughs and bounce rates—and with good reason. Today, consumers' expectations are as high as their patience is short. They want their answers now and they refuse to endure delays. Buyers and tenants in a shifted market aren't all that different: They know the deck is stacked in their favor, and if doing a deal requires extra time, effort, or expense, the prospect will either punish you on price or simply look elsewhere for a truly motivated seller.

Your new mantra is, "Make it easy to make a deal!" Map out and avoid all the foreseeable pitfalls, such as environmental issues or covenants or restrictions on the property. Make credible, detailed information about the property readily available, particularly on your website. Go above and beyond with information. For example:

1. Have blueprints, maintenance records, demographic information, and other relevant information at the ready in any and every format prospects might demand. Have it on your website; be ready to email it, fax it, or ship it; and have hard copies at the property to review during tours and open houses.

2. Offer to do the extra research or analysis they need to make a final decision. This can often be the difference between closing the transaction or not.

> *The level of service and credible information you provide will determine if you are going to get the next deal from the client.*
> Reagan Dixon,
> Dallas, Texas

3. Research local demand data and market information. This is especially valuable in retail where you can often determine the specific type of business the property would best suit. Then, prepare a marketing presentation of the data to promote the specifics of how this retail segment could benefit from the location.

4. Provide a list of other companies in the area with which the client may already do business. Again, locations are evaluated in part by how convenient they make it to work there. Likewise, if a prospect will share the information, illustrate how the new location will impact employee commutes, which is a huge factor in employee retention and satisfaction.

5. Provide offer forms or standardized contracts that you know the seller would accept. Does your state have promulgated or standardized commercial forms? This knowledge makes it easier for the buyer to make an offer that has a better chance of being accepted.

The great American businessman William Clement Stone once said, "Sales are contingent upon the attitude of the salesman, not the attitude of the prospect." Staging is all about attitude—your vision for a property and your belief in the opportunities it represents. In a shifting market or under difficult conditions, there is no excuse not to use the strategies we've outlined here to your advantage. You know the competition for the attention of qualified buyers and tenants is more intense than ever in a shift. Your only option is to differentiate your properties and demonstrate their value, show the vision to potential clients, and build the strong relationships required to make the transactions happen.

TACTIC #9
CREATE URGENCY – OVERCOMING BUYER AND TENANT RELUCTANCE

A simple rule dictates my buying: Be fearful when others are greedy, and be greedy when others are fearful.

Warren Buffett

The jury is out on the value (or lack thereof) of financial advisers: Do they improve portfolio performance or not? The experts can't seem to agree, but a recent study did uncover one key role advisers play. When investors' emotions are running high and they are more likely to make decisions that aren't in their best interests in the long term, advisers are often a stabilizing force, counseling them not to aggressively buy or sell in the wake of market volatility. Philip Z. Maymin and Gregg S. Fisher, in a Spring 2011 article in *The Journal of Wealth Management*, explained their findings: "The adviser's role in helping investors stay disciplined and on plan in the face of market volatility . . . is one that is highly valued by the individual investor."

An expert commercial real estate broker offers the same value to his clients in a shifted market. But rather than cautioning them against taking action, he should spur them on.

Buyers and tenants in a shifted market often understand that they hold the power. Yet they still hold back, refusing to leverage it. Oftentimes, they believe that there's another, better deal to be had if they look a bit more or wait a bit longer. They are fearful of making a bad decision, either because of uncertainties in the real estate market and economic environment, because of their inability to trust in their broker's counsel, or because what they're really looking for is a "steal." They believe that the market may drop just a bit more, and they don't want to invest in a property that may continue to lose value or miss an opportunity to get a slightly better price. This saps your time and energy and often results in buyers and tenants missing out on the best opportunities *for them*.

It falls to you to save them from themselves, to overcome this fear and reluctance, not because it's in your best interests to do so, but because it's usually in your clients' best interests. When you represent investors and tenants, it's your job to negotiate the best deal on the property that best meets their needs. Unfortunately, it can be difficult to convince them that that is exactly what you've done.

We've addressed techniques for highlighting value and overcoming buyer and tenant reluctance from the seller and landlord perspectives in the previous tactics. When you are representing investors and tenants, your strategy should be twofold:

1. Become your client's economist of choice and educate them on market and business realities.

2. Help them tap into their "why" to highlight opportunities ready for the taking.

Focus on your clients' business needs rather than simply on transactions, and you will showcase yourself as the expert they can trust to help them make a wise, informed decision.

1. BECOME THE ECONOMIST OF CHOICE

"Do you think this is the bottom of the market?" We all hate that question, one we hear often from our clients in a shifted market. From the seasoned investor to the owner of a small start-up company new to commercial real estate, they all want your expert opinion. But what they are really asking, of course, is "Should I buy now or wait a bit longer?"

It's great when they turn to you for advice. It's exactly what you want them to do—recognize your expertise. The problem is that you can't tell them whether or not this is the absolute bottom, and they likely just want you to confirm their suspicions that they should hold out. If you could identify the bottom of the market, you'd be clairvoyant. No one has a crystal ball. The only way we know when we've reached the absolute bottom is in hindsight, when the market has begun to improve. Then we can look back and say, "Right there. That was the bottom." It can be a very short-lived moment. Once it passes, the best deals disappear and buyers and tenants flood the market, competing to take advantage of the low before it becomes a high. That's a great time for you as a broker, when more clients are looking to do more transactions, but you don't want your current clients to wait that long and lose out on the best opportunities now. Robert Tufts, managing director in New Orleans, Louisiana, has built an investment portfolio on this strategy. "We attempt to buy commercial properties during the economic downturns. This gives us a competitive advantage in the market to be able to make lease deals that other landlords simply cannot match."

So you must distract them from the idea of the market bottoming out. Warren Buffett often says that investors should try to be "fearful when others are greedy, and be greedy when others are fearful." Shortly after the nuclear disasters in Japan in 2011, where do you think Warren Buffett was? In Japan, that's where. That is the mindset you should try to instill in your clients. Sam Zell once said, "Fear and courage are very closely related. Anybody who does not understand fear does not know courage." Help your clients understand their fear so that they can be courageous. To shift their perspective, focus their attention on the stellar deals available right now and the long-term effects of taking advantage of those deals in terms of return on investment and cash flow. Show them a graph of local or regional commercial prices over time and explain it to them. Tell them, "The market is down 50 percent from recent highs and 30 percent historically. This is a great time to buy."

If you are dealing with investors, it's crucial to focus on the long-term returns, not the short-term concerns. Investors have one goal: Use assets effectively to earn as high a return as possible while minimizing risk. When they have funds sitting in a poor-performing investment vehicle somewhere, they need to reposition funds as fast as possible to start earning a better return. And commercial real estate in a shifted market is an ideal opportunity. "We may go lower," you can explain, "but your capital is going to sit in low—return investments earning a few basis points, when it could be generating significant cash flow. There's still a slight downward risk, but there's a great potential upside if and when properties return to historical pricing trends." Encourage them to look at other points of analysis. Is the price below replacement cost? What is the potential for cash flow? How could the cash flow be utilized? What other investment opportunities could it support? Dissuade them from waiting for a few more percentage points on the return, and persuade them to use their capital to its best use right now, particularly if they're holding a lot of cash and cash equivalents—assets that aren't earning more than a couple of percentage points anyway.

Important note! Anytime you are discussing projected returns with a client, be sure to include a clear disclaimer that what you are discussing are projections and estimations only, not guarantees. This is essential for anything you put in writing.

If your client is a portfolio investor, you can also focus on the fact that taking advantage of a current opportunity doesn't prohibit them from taking advantage of another possibly better opportunity in the near future, an approach similar to the financial concept of dollar cost averaging. The slightly smaller overall return on the first property will be balanced by the greater return on another. Maybe they would be interested in using some capital to take advantage of an opportunity now and more capital in a few months to make another, possibly better, investment. They just keep taking swings at the bottom in the hopes of earning the best overall returns possible. In the early stages of a shifted market, this hedge approach works well, particularly if it seems fairly definite that the downward trend will continue.

Just remember, savvy investors would rather buy right than sell right—and buying in a shift is buying right.

If a buyer is worried that prices are still spiraling downward and can't make a decision on a property, ask them to look at the price and see what it means in their business model. Is the price below replacement cost? Is it a good deal regardless? Are rates going to continue to go lower? If you think that the market is going to drop further, write a counteroffer.

Nancy Lemas,
Boise, Idaho

For your tenant clients, focus on cash flow. Every month they delay making a move is a month that they are paying more rent than they should be, a month when their balance sheet could be improved—now and for a number of years. Rather than think about the market continuing to trend downward, get them focused on what an opportunity would mean to the strength of their business, how the savings could be invested elsewhere or used to cover downward trending sales. In a shifted market, there are landlords clamoring for tenants, willing to buy out leases and make vast concessions to get them to move. Remind your clients of these market realities often.

To help your clients trust in the advice you offer, tell them, "I'm your commercial property expert. As soon as I find a good property, I'll let you and a few others know about it in advance." Then, scour the market for the best properties available to send to various segments of your client list, and when you do send them, include a minianalysis of the property and its characteristics. While you need to make sure that these are bona fide deals, they don't have to be your listings, and they don't have to be perfect properties. The most important part of this communication is your analysis of the properties' potential. You're not necessarily trying to sell these specific properties, you're just giving your clients confidence that you know a great deal when you see one. This will help them trust you when you present them with a specific property that is an ideal fit.

As their economist of choice, the most important thing to demonstrate to your buyers or tenants is this key fact: They should be afraid to make a decision in the marketplace without your expert advice and counsel.

Kristan Cole has a small network of seventy-five business owners, executives, and board members from local companies and civic institutions

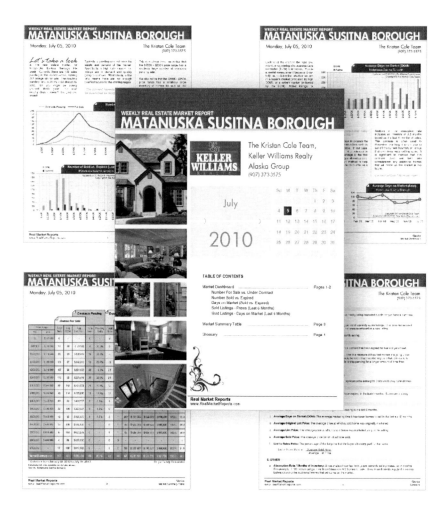

Figure 27 - Kristan Cole's newsletter

that have commercial needs. She calls them her "stat group." Every month, she sends them her market update—a focused list of key metrics including volume, units, days on market, and average sales price (presented as quarterly, year-to-date, and year-over-year numbers). She also includes notices of default: "It's like a ninety-day preview on foreclosures and a leading indicator of the health of the market. Over time, you can see trends forming," she explained. The metrics are sent to her by a title company, and her team simply reformats them and sends them out. She rarely markets properties to this group, and yet many of her leads come from them: "I became known as the expert and now they seek me out." She became the economist of choice in her market and has leveraged it to great success.

2. TAP INTO THEIR WHY

Problems—every client has them. In this case, said client is working with you because they believe you can help solve them. Yet when the solution is revealed from your magical hands, they can't seem to accept it. You must leverage what you know about the client—tap into their why—to help them seize the opportunity before them.

Every buyer or tenant has a reason for buying or leasing in a shifted market, when times are uncertain. There is either a pressing business concern or they recognize the wisdom of taking advantage of a down market. Either way, you must clearly map the opportunities you present to their business needs, which you should have clarified during the conversion process. Help them clarify exactly what it is they are looking for. Create a form you can use to outline the property attributes they require or that meet their needs. Then, when you find a property that has those features, you can use the form to create a point-by-point presentation of how the property meets or exceeds those needs.

For buyers, typically the economics of a particular opportunity are the highlight, what helps them decide to take action. But that doesn't mean they don't have additional motivations. For business buyers, there may be prestige and pride in having grown large enough to purchase a building rather than lease space, and an ideal property may help in recruiting or showcasing the business in terms of location or quality. Or they may see an opportunity with an SBA loan to reduce their occupancy costs by investing in an affordable building, utilizing the majority of the space (at least 51 percent) and leasing the remainder. In today's shifted market, with low valuations and interest rates, the buy vs. lease analysis, which we discuss in more detail in Tactic #10, for many small businesses is decidedly weighted to "buy."

Owning a property is also an investment in a long-term asset that can be leveraged for a variety of portfolio purposes including retirement income, estate planning, legacy building, and so on. At the very least, it's smart asset allocation in a time when other financial vehicles are either unstable or offering a miniscule return.

A shifted market is a great time if you are a tenant. For most of these clients, the why of looking for new opportunities (if not driven by a broader business decision, such as relocating headquarters) is typically to find a better space (either nicer or closer to a particular geographic area or with better amenities) or to lower costs. Opportunities to do either or both are rampant, and they should understand that. To help your clients move on these opportunities, highlight the following points when appropriate:

1. In a shifted market, tenants can upgrade from a C or B property to a B or A property at close to the same price point. Or they can upgrade to more space without increasing costs.

2. Landlords are more than willing to help tenants find a space that better fits their needs—less space, more space, different kinds of space, or more flexibility to expand or contract—rather than lose them.

3. If you would like to move; particularly to lower your costs, but your lease isn't up for another year or so and your current landlord won't renegotiate; other landlords may be willing to buy out your lease to entice you into a new space.

4. When moving or renegotiating a lease, tenants have the opportunity to push to lock in rates for as long as possible and negotiate fixed price renewal options—they can actually get a long-term lease with short-term options. While landlords will be working hard to keep below-market lease terms short, they are driven to get and keep tenants and may be willing to negotiate longer-term leases.

5. If renegotiating a lease, they can negotiate a reduction in their space and then "blend and extend." When the economy is shifting, many tenants are reducing headcount and need less square footage. You should also work to remove personal liability from the lease for your tenant clients.

6. As we discussed in Tactic #7, concessions are often as high as the market is low in a shift, so tenants have the power to negotiate for all sorts of value-added points such as moving costs, build-outs, options to expand into other space when it becomes available, options to contract the space leased based on the performance of the business, a "burndown" of their financial liability or security deposit, and so on.

When capital is tied up in high rents or sitting under mattresses or in low-yield bank accounts or treasury bonds, that money wants to come out of lower-yielding investments and enter into higher-yielding ones. Be the expert adviser your clients need: Help them overcome their internal hurdles, use their leverage to negotiate a deal that's right for them, and realize the benefits of acting wisely in a shifted market.

TACTIC #10
EXPAND THE OPTIONS –
CREATIVE FINANCING

Life is constantly providing us with new funds,
new resources, even when we are reduced to immobility.
In life's ledger there is no such thing as frozen assets.

HENRY MILLER

During the run-up to the residential real estate collapse in the mid-2000s, lax lending standards sadly became the norm. Everyone was caught up in the rush to cash in on a red-hot real estate market. If you had a credit score and a pulse, the thinking went, you could get a home loan. In fact, as Alex Blumberg on NPR's award-winning *The Giant Pool of Money* broadcast pointed out, "Actually, that pulse thing—also optional. Like the case in Ohio where twenty-three dead people were approved for mortgages." While commercial lending never reached these depths, credit and capital were "free-flowing." Funding for a property purchase—either through conventional loans, venture capital, or commercial mortgage-backed security markets—was easy to find and easy to access. Investors had only to provide minimal equity to get maximized loans; 20/80 paper was the norm, and 10/90 wasn't unheard of. The market was on its way up, and everybody wanted in on the action.

And then it all changed—just as it has many times before and will again in the future. The difference is that with legislation mandating restrictions on lending and borrowing, the credit and capital landscape may never be what it was in this heyday; money may never be that easily obtained again. What's left is the new norm: credit rating requirements are higher, even for hard-money lenders, and at least 30 to 40 percent equity investment is a requirement for most conventional financing—equity that many investors or businesses can't or don't want to supply. When the equity requirement doubles, the cash-on-cash return is cut in half and you have to part with more of your precious cash, making real estate investing potentially less appealing.

As a broker, to survive a shift, you have to put deals together. But if funding for those deals is harder to access, what can you do? Our best advice is to align yourself with the people and institutions who do have the funds to lend, who are open to creative solutions, and who recognize the opportunity in the current market. Build a diverse finance team around you and put creative financing to use whenever you can.

Of course, first and foremost, that means working with prospects and clients who have the funding to complete a transaction. The most important people in your database right now are buyers with cash in hand, typically high net-worth individuals, venture capital groups, managed real estate investment funds, and other individuals and businesses ready and financially able to take advantage of the market. These investors are looking for margin and leverage, an opportunity to earn a better return than is possible by holding cash. They also see commercial real estate as potentially more secure than what the stock market may have to offer. Unfortunately, there are fewer and fewer of them ready to enter the market. As Christopher Perez, director of Oceanview Financial, said, "Money is like energy: It can't be created or destroyed. So it hasn't disappeared, it's just being held in deep pockets." The competition for those who are ready to enter the market is fierce, so you must also identify other potential sources of funds and get creative in how you tap into them.

In a shift, particularly when the economic environment is poor, pursue prospects, properties, and networks that can help you tap into nonconventional sources of funds, particularly those outlined in figure 28.

NONCONVENTIONAL SOURCES OF FUNDS IN A SHIFT

1. Small Business Administration (SBA) loans

2. International investors

3. Owner financing

4. Private lenders

5. Institutional lenders

Figure 28

Of course, when you step outside of conventional financing, what you find may be a little shocking. The money that gets us through a shift is typically hard money. In Dante's *The Divine Comedy*, usurers were relegated to the seventh circle of hell. When charging interest became legal in the sixteenth century, usury came to mean charging an interest rate above the legal limit. Obviously, perspectives have shifted. Yet people still cast a hard eye on hard-money lenders . . . sometimes for good reason.

Time and again, in our conversations about hard money with those in commercial real estate and finance, we heard, "You need to be cautious." Because hard money is the most likely source of fraud in the world of finance, and in tough markets, even above-board lenders are offering stringent, if not brutal, terms (double-digit interest on one- or two-year notes).

You need to be certain that you can make the property valuable enough in time to pay off the note, or you'll be in trouble.
Vikki Keyser,
Sarasota, Florida

The problem is that hard-money lenders take risks others won't. The upside is that they are a source of capital when other sources run dry; the downside is they need to cover their risk with above-market interest rates. The best use of hard money is to bridge the equity gap, using short-term loans that can be covered by the cash flow generated or the increase in the value of the property due to improvements in the first year or two. But anybody considering such a loan must carefully analyze the terms, because if the note comes due and payment can't be made, the lender likely has the right to take ownership of the property, even if they only put up 20 percent of the capital in the transaction.

As we said in the last tactic, there is always capital waiting to be invested—sitting in low-yield investment vehicles and waiting to be turned to a better use with a higher return. But you may need to expand your search and be prepared for different criteria. Your job is to find the money and discover the parameters that will make it move. In a hot market, a commercial broker may not need to assist their buyers with capital sources, but in a shifted one, brokers may have to help with funding sources as well as finding quality properties.

1. SMALL BUSINESS ADMINISTRATION LOANS

In times of recession, the federal government is usually quick to step in with programs and services to stimulate the economy. Small businesses and entrepreneurial start-ups create domestic jobs, sell products and services locally, and pay federal and state taxes, so stimulus money is often channeled to them. The commercial real estate sector is not forgotten in these programs.

In particular, the Small Business Administration offers what I call "killer paper" for businesses that want to purchase office, industrial, or retail properties for their own use. The SBA works with lenders to offer low-equity, low-interest, long-term notes—terms a business may not be able to find anywhere else, even in a strong capital market. The 504 and 7(a) SBA loan programs are inviting for banks and business owners. Banks carry less risk because the SBA partners with a certified development company (CDC) that underwrites as much as 40 percent of the loan, while guaranteeing that the bank gets paid first if there is a default. The business owner is happy because they get fantastic terms with as little as 10 percent down. The main hitch is that the owner must occupy at least 51 percent of the property.

Nancy Lemas, of Boise, Idaho, learned in the last shift that it didn't matter what you were selling: if the banks weren't lending, a deal couldn't get done. In 2008, she saw that banks were hesitating to fund speculative investment in commercial real estate. Having always fostered good relationships with bankers, she asked them directly, "What types of loans are you making?" The banks weren't willing to absorb risk or had such a substantial commercial portfolio that additional loans wouldn't work for their balance sheets. However, they were eager to offer new SBA loan programs that mitigated the risk through federal government guarantees and created a class of owner-occupied commercial assets.

Nancy quickly learned everything she could about how these programs worked, how to process the complicated paperwork, and what the benefits of the program were to owner-users, to banks, and to commercial brokers like her. She educated herself and then leveraged her experience as a tenant representative and in purchasing owner-user properties to identify tenants who might be interested in purchasing their business location. For office and retail properties you bring to the market, turn to the current tenants and to the broader tenant population for possible buyers.

Butch West, of Austin, Texas, is approached by lenders with SBA programs on a weekly basis. "There's an abundance of SBA lenders. The reality is that most small investors aren't ready to enter the market, either because of lack of capital or fear. They look at their cash flow and ask, 'Can we cover a 90 percent loan?'" As a broker, you have to help them get past any unfounded fears by running the numbers and comparing their current tenant situation with an ownership scenario. Prepare a lease vs. purchase analysis, like the one shown in figure 29, to make a compelling financial case. You can download a template spreadsheet from www.KellerInk. com/SHIFTCommercial. (Remember, never present pro forma projections to a client without a clear disclaimer, like the one in the figure.)

"I believe this is one of the best times in recent history for small businesses to be purchasing their facilities rather than renting," said Nancy. Her pitch to tenants is, "Why wouldn't you want to save money now by purchasing through this government program? You're currently paying

LEASE VS. PURCHASE ANALYSIS

PURCHASE OCCUPANCY COST OF ONLY $0.67 PER SQ. FT. PER MONTH VS. $0.88 TO LEASE

Building total sq. ft.:	20,000
Owner occupied space:	20,000
Sales Price:	$3,000,000
Down Payment %:	20%
Down Payment $:	$300,000
Loan Amount:	$2,700,000
Interest Rate:	6.00%
Amortization Years:	10
Building Gross Rental Income:	$15
Estimated Operating Expenses/CAMs:	$5

Purchase

Loan Amount	$2,700,000
Annual Debt Service Expense (1)	$233,431
(+) Plus Estimated Operating Expenses/CAMs	$100,000
(=) Equals Subtotal Annual Debt Service Exp.	$333,431
(-) Minus Avg. Annual Principal Paydown (1)	$28,012
(=) Equals Net Pretax Debt Service Exp.	$305,419
(-) Minus Applicable Annual Tax Savings (2)	$145,358
(=) Equals Effective Annual Debt Service Exp.	$160,061
Divided by 12 = Effective Monthly Debt Service Exp.	$13,338
Divided by S.F. = Total Cost per S.F. for Owner/User	**$0.67**

Lease

Annual Lease Expense	$480,000
(-) Minus CAMs $0.45 per S.F.	$100,000
(-) Minus Applicable Annual Tax Savings (3)	$168,000
(=) Equals Effective Annual Lease Exp.	$212,000
Divided by 12 = Effective Monthly Lease Exp.	$17,667
Divided by S.F. = Total Cost per S.F. for Lease	**$0.88**

Note: The broker makes no representations or warranties as to the validity of this information or the implications of this form. Please consult with a tax specialist regarding the possible tax benefits.
1. Average annual principle paydown based on 5 years accumulation.
2. Assumes applicable 35% effective tax rate (combined state and federal) plus deduction for depreciation based on 39-year schedule.
3. Assumes applicable 35% tax rate (combined state and federal).
Loan terms and conditions may vary based on lending program, subsidiary, and applicant qualification.

Figure 29

rent at $20 per square foot, but that cost would drop to $12 a square foot if you purchased this building. Plus, it allows you to build equity in an owned real estate investment vs. simply paying rent, thus offering you an extra succession plan/retirement plan element. And if you sell your business, you can lease back the property."

If you can find quality tenants, small business loan opportunities are plentiful and totally accessible. Pursue tenants, use the conversion approaches we discussed in Tactic #8, and discuss with small business owners that now is the right time to buy.

2. INTERNATIONAL INVESTORS

About twenty years ago, I was in Germany when I saw the car of my dreams: the Porsche 911 Targa. At home, I hadn't considered actually buying one because they were simply too expensive, but I decided to ask about the car anyway. When the dealer told me the price, I couldn't believe it: It was 18,000 deutschemarks. At the time, the dollar was so strong compared to the mark that it worked out to approximately 7,000 U.S. dollars. I had to pay 1,000 U.S. dollars to import it, but I still paid only about 45 percent of what I would have had I purchased the car domestically. I even sold the car five years later for 16,000 U.S. dollars.

Today, the reverse is true. As much as I hate to admit it, the United States of America is on sale to foreign investors. Although the U.S. recession and shifted market are not unique in the global marketplace, the heavily discounted property prices and the weakened dollar (against many foreign currencies) combine to create a double discount for foreign investors who have capital on hand to invest. They have increased buying power and the potential ROI is high, making it a perfect time for them to buy. The world is flat and getting flatter, or so says Thomas Friedman, and foreign investors are ever more likely to leverage stronger currencies to maximize their return on investments in foreign countries, not just the United States. The truth of this tactic is that when the commercial market is slumping and local currency is weak, international investors often come calling and should be targeted by smart brokers.

When we spoke with John Aucamp, managing director, International Investor Services in Sherman Oaks, California, he had just returned from a trip to Geneva, Switzerland, where he met with institutional investors and wealthy individuals to discuss investment opportunities in commercial properties in the United States. The meetings were set up through friends who knew the investors were interested in commercial real estate and who knew John specialized in investment-grade properties. He quickly found himself in competition with other top brokerage firms and learned that the investors were doing their due diligence, fact-checking everything that John told them. With high-caliber investors, you should expect to be competing with others for their attention, and you should expect them to be well-informed. They are looking for highly credible, experienced brokers who offer the highest level of ethics and service.

John's experience has also shown that it takes a significant amount of work to develop relationships with international investors. It is more difficult for these individuals, who may have limited contacts and access to information in the market where they are investing, to directly verify projected market conditions, local economic factors, neighborhood trends, comparative sales, and other supporting details. They have no choice but to rely heavily on their brokers, and so brokers must be vetted very carefully. But while the process of developing a relationship with a potential international client can be intensive, once trust is gained, it is easily maintained and less likely to be captured by a competitor.

Relationship building with some international investors may also require developing deep knowledge of a culture or language in order to provide the highest level of service. Along the southern border of the United States, there are tremendous opportunities to sell properties to investors from Mexico. Rhonda and Butch West, of Austin, Texas, have found that this class of investment sales is an area of positive growth. They have hired expatriates to help with sales to Mexican cash buyers. "The keys to this business are to be able to speak the language natively, know the culture, and develop the relationships," explained Rhonda. The Wests then foster those relationships with service. They provide all the information the buyers need to make them feel comfortable in the buyers' language. By providing this highest level of service, they are building repeat business.

Additionally, international investors will want to partner with someone on the ground locally who can also provide comprehensive services before, during, and after the transaction. They need brokers to demonstrate a commitment to be there for them now and in the future. If they invest with you, they may want you to oversee the management of the property for the duration of their investment. Are you prepared to do that? In Tactic #12, we will discuss the importance of developing a fully consultative approach in your brokerage, offering a variety of services that you can leverage now and in an improving market.

Position yourself as a conduit and trusted adviser for foreign investors to take advantage of the international investment property gold rush that may be coming. To tap into these investors, leverage the following advice:

1. Make contacts and develop relationships with accountants, attorneys, financial advisers, and other professional service groups who already serve international clients. Residential real estate agents who handle luxury homes and high-end condominium sales are also a good referral source, as foreign investors may first purchase second homes in the market that interests them.

2. Be prepared to travel to meet with potential investors. It shows your commitment to developing a relationship and your accessibility. Make it easy for them to work with you.

3. Position yourself as a consultant and adviser rather than a salesperson. Add value to the relationship through your knowledge and research of the commercial markets. Partner with your clients' existing legal, accounting, and banking teams to provide cohesive and unified advice for their commercial investments.

4. Read the foreign financial press for insight into the desirability of U.S. commercial real estate. This is also an excellent way to spot potential investors, a favored method by investment banks for spotting business opportunities.

5. Understand their investment intent and objectives: Is this a long-term investment or a speculative one? Either way, if you can satisfy their requirements for service, then repeat business will be there for you.

6. Always assume that you are competing and be prepared to deliver the highest level of trust and service. If you are unwilling or unprepared

to deliver the level of service required for major foreign investors, consider partnering with other brokers experienced in working with them.

7. Develop your knowledge of the regulatory environments in which an international investor functions, both domestically and across borders. In commercial real estate, the foreign regulatory environment may actually be quite onerous, creating an additional incentive for an international investor.

Begin now and look beyond your borders, outside your typical sphere, to find foreign investors who have the funds and the motivation to complete commercial transactions today.

3. OWNER FINANCING

Value-add and specialized-use properties may be some of the hardest types of properties to finance in a shifted market. So when Butch West got multiple offers on a marina that needed some love, he was excited. And the fact that two offers met the owner's terms exactly surprised him. There was one catch, as there always seems to be: The two prospective buyers needed owner financing to complete the deal. On value-add or specialized-use properties in particular, financing can be difficult to obtain or lenders will only offer up a small portion of the total purchase price. For these properties, owner financing can be the best way to put a deal together. Unfortunately for Butch, the owner was not open to the idea, and the property still hasn't sold.

While owner financing may not be readily available in a shift—because owners who have strong equity in a property aren't likely selling in a down market—you never know what opportunities may come your way. Often, prospective buyers may need owner financing on a small portion of the price, maybe 10 or 20 percent, to reduce the equity needed up front or to bridge the gap between the asking price and what a lender will put up for the property. And for some properties, owner financing may be the best way to ensure that the owner gets what they need, according to Rhonda West. "Owner financing is an answer for people who don't need to take a lot of equity out, but need to get out of the property. For instance, with land, it might be worth their while to do owner financing short term to get out of the real estate taxes until the buyer can refinance."

Early in your relationship, have a frank and open discussion with your clients to explore the possibility of owner financing, advises Cliff Bogart, CCIM, a veteran of the Houston, Dallas, and Austin, Texas, commercial real estate markets. "If the loan component is going to be in the 50 to 60 percent range, ask if the owner could finance 20 to 30 percent so that buyers could come in with the remaining 20 percent equity. Explain that it would open the property to a bigger pool of potential investors." Educate your clients—talk about the various options they might consider. Probe to find out what they really need to walk away with, what their short-term vs. long-term needs are.

A pharmacist near Oxnard, California, owned a store property that happened to be the last piece of real estate a developer needed to create a new shopping plaza. The pharmacist was asking $1.4 million, but the buyer would only offer $800,000. The deal seemed to be in deadlock until Chris Sands stepped in and found a way to make both sides happy.

He began by probing for pain: What was it both sides really wanted? What he discovered was that the pharmacist wanted to retire and needed to supplement her retirement income by about $3,500 per month. The developer really couldn't offer more than $800,000 because of all other expenses and cash outlays that would be required to develop the property. Once he understood the reality of the situation, it wasn't hard to identify a solution.

Chris structured an owner-financing deal whereby the developer paid only $150,000 up front to cover all of the commissions and closing costs, and agreed to pay $3,500 per month for ten years with a balloon payment of $850,000 in the tenth year. This equated to a 5 percent loan for the developer and a lot of freed-up cash to use in developing the property. The property sale allowed the pharmacist to retire comfortably and the developer to have the funds needed to improve the property.

In a shifted market, you may have to be just as creative in developing a financing solution as Chris was. Because the terms of owner financing are infinitely flexible, you may find that an owner who is forced to sell in a down market could still earn a strong return by creating a unique financing model. From balloon payments to leasing options with a "fixed price" in three to five years, when it comes to owner financing, almost anything is possible.

4. PRIVATE LENDERS

Private lenders are often the only source of funding for some transactions. However, they often loan money with hard terms, so all of the cautions raised at the beginning of this tactic apply. They are entirely unregulated, so borrowers must do their due diligence: Research the lender and have legal counsel review all contracts carefully. All of that said, private lenders who follow legal loan practices—and that defines the majority of them—are key sources of funding in a shift.

One option for leveraging relationships with private lenders is to consider the possibility of a "credit enhancement" arrangement. For lenders with cash to cover more than just the equity commitment of conventional financing, but who can't qualify because of poor credit, credit enhancements can be a good option. Typically, a private lender will sign on the note as a guarantor

For those that have liquidity and credit issues, there are private lenders. But you really need to be concerned about the terms and who these lenders are.

Rhonda West,
Austin, Texas

for a point or two of the sale price; however, that also allows them to pick up first-place position in case of loan default, even though they've invested no capital. Some well-established estate funds often play this role. But this is also an area fraught with potential fraud, so extreme caution is absolutely necessary.

If your client is working with a private lender and you see red flags of fraud or terms that your client isn't likely to meet, it is your fiduciary responsibility to advise them to look elsewhere. Christopher Perez, Philadelphia, Pennsylvania, recommends watching for the following signs that a lender isn't a "real" lender:

1. Beware of anyone charging commitment fees, due diligence fees, and the like. Real lenders typically do not charge these fees. The standard cost of an appraisal is about all a borrower should have to pay out of pocket.

2. A surefire sign that someone isn't a real lender is issuing interest letters or letters of intent with little-to-no due diligence or underwriting. When a real lender issues an offer, they plan on lending that amount of money—the funds have been allocated in their systems. They won't make that move unless they've already completed their underwriting.

3. If the lender isn't public, if it is difficult to find information about them through public records, or if they can't provide references from other borrowers or proof that they've handled similar loans in the past, you should probably walk away.

The reality is it's the private and other hard-money lenders who typically help us through a shift, so help your clients explore this option by identifying the "real" lenders in your market.

5. INSTITUTIONAL FUNDS

Hedge fund, thy name is mud.

Unfortunately, investment events of the mid-2000s have soured most individuals—and regulators—on certain forms of funding that were common just a few years ago, including hedge fund loans and commercial mortgage-backed securities (CMBS). Yet these types of funds are slowly coming back into the market, and in the coming years, they are likely to expand—possibly rapidly. In fact, institutional funds could be the market's saving grace.

"These days, large transactions are often paid for with cash. And that cash is not coming out of people's pockets," explains Christopher

Perez. Butch West agrees. "The last few large transactions we did were paid for in cash, but the cash was alluded to as 'Wall Street money.'" Nobody wants to use the term hedge fund anymore—the connotations are too negative.

These types of vehicles are poised to play an important role in the coming years. The statistics for banks are frightening, to say the least. There were 140 bank failures in 2009, 157 in 2010, and 48 in the first six months of 2011. By the end of 2013, more than $1 trillion in commercial loans will balloon, possibly causing an avalanche of bank failures. Jon D. Greenlee, associate director of the Division of Banking Supervision and Regulation for the Federal Reserve, explained why in his congressional testimony in 2009: "In addition to losses caused by declining property cash flows and deteriorating conditions for construction loans, losses will also be boosted by the depreciating collateral value underlying those maturing loans. The losses will place continued pressure on banks' earnings, especially those of smaller regional and community banks that have high concentrations of CRE (commercial real estate) loans. The current fundamental weakness in CRE markets is exacerbated by the fact that the CMBS market, which previously had financed about 30 percent of all commercial originations and completed construction projects, has remained closed since the start of the crisis." Conditions have begun to improve, but the outlook is still not rosy; the Federal Reserve believes that financial institutions will continue to see substantial commercial real estate losses through 2013. What those banks need now is a way to clean up their books. That's where institutional funds, particularly CMBS and hedge funds, come in.

"CMBS has reawakened for higher-quality deals," says Cliff Bogart. "And that also allows lenders to sell notes and free up capital that they can lend to new investors." And Christopher Perez, who is launching a new hedge fund, believes that funds like his may save some banks. "Imagine that the end of a quarter is coming up and it's looking terrible for a bank because of auditor scrutiny. If the bank could call me and say, 'Can you take some of this portfolio off my hands,' that would save the bank and provide a sound investment vehicle for people."

For brokers, what all of this means is that institutional money is coming back into the market. Some hedge funds will be willing to make loans to investors who wouldn't qualify for a conventional loan. "Bankers aren't entrepreneurial; they're actuarial," explained Christopher. "Whereas hedge funds often rely on old-fashioned underwriting, looking at the whole picture rather than just a checklist that doesn't necessarily tell you much about the borrower." That said, institutional money can be hard money too, so borrowers must be cautious.

Again, brokers can align themselves with organizations that are entering the market. Unfortunately, says Christopher, "Wall Street is a very private place. Most times you're either 'in the know' or not." He recommends the following tactics for breaking through the barriers:

1. To find the "real money" start with the brand-name houses first. If you have a client working with a Wall Street investment source, ask for a connection. If you know of one that has turned down a client, contact them and ask who they know who might say yes. These referrals can be gold. You may have to run through this process many times over, so be persistent.

2. Keep track of the transactions that are closing. Go to those brokers and find out where the funding came from. It can be hard to find the answer, but if you leverage your network, you'll be able to access this information.

3. Look to trade magazines, like the *Scotsman Guide*, for information about who's entering the market and for what types of projects.

Identify the best lenders with the most diverse lending criteria to help clients and prospects connect with the funds they need.

WHO NEEDS YOUR HELP

In Tactic #11, we will talk about quality properties as a market of the moment. Quality investors are the prospects of the moment. You want to pursue them, but if they have cash to invest, it's unlikely that they need your help identifying creative financing options to get a deal done. Although, you never know what can happen in a shift: An investor who seems top tier on paper may need more help than you might think once you get into a transaction.

But the people who will really need your guidance, your advice, your expertise, and your connections will be smaller investors. "Lenders are trying to get the word out that money is available," explained Chuck Frankel of New York, New York. "But the underwriting criteria are tough. Many lenders have money, but are only offering it on select quality deals. It's not going to be there for smaller investors who are looking for financing on a value-add or improvement property that is a discount buy. Or if it is, they're going to have to put up a lot of equity. That said, while conventional funding is harder to come by, it's at historically low interest rates. So although they may have to come up with more equity, they're getting a deal on the interest expense."

If you are representing a value-add property or if you have an investor who is looking for a great discounted deal, be prepared to discuss creative financing options from the very first meeting. Value your cash investors and make sure you are offering the highest service possible so that you retain them. And leverage your network to align yourself with the best lenders in the market. This knowledge will only deepen the expertise you offer to clients and it will help you take advantage of markets of the moment.

As a broker, you should identify the best lenders in your market. Do your own due diligence, make connections with these lenders, and discover who their target customers are. That way, if you see a client struggling with equity requirements or credit issues, you can help them identify all possible solutions. It is an important service you can provide to your buyer clients, but it also helps you expand the market of buyers for your seller clients.

TACTIC #11
MASTER THE MARKET
OF THE MOMENT –
IDENTIFY AND ESTABLISH
NEEDED EXPERTISE

The survival of the fittest is the ageless law of nature,
but the fittest are rarely the strong. The fittest are those endowed
with the qualifications for adaptation, the ability to accept the
inevitable and conform to the unavoidable, to harmonize with
existing or changing conditions.

DAVE E. SMALLEY

In Spencer Johnson's classic book *Who Moved My Cheese?*, the tiny human Haw inscribes a message for his friend Hem: "If you do not change, you can become extinct." If you're among the millions who've read this popular fable, you'll remember that Haw had come to accept the fact that the cheese was gone and that he'd have to adapt in order to survive. And he was trying to encourage his pal to do the same. For all of our talk of specialization, the truth remains that if all your commercial success was pooled in an area that the shift has effectively dried up, you too must heed Haw's timeless advice. Every market holds opportunities, small pockets of business that arise from the ashes and which sometimes become significant new sources of income. To capture the opportunities that exist in these markets of the moment, you must be willing to adapt and diversify your brokerage practice.

I spoke with one top-tier investment-focused broker who told me flat out that they would only handle investment sales and that his office doesn't waste time with smaller transactions. Well, the current shift is only remarkable in the fact that investment sales have been even harder hit than usual. Credit almost always contracts in a shift, and investment sales are often the first and hardest hit. I was not surprised when he later shared that their commission income had declined by 90 percent and they'd had to lay off most of their brokers. In a shift, you must adjust or risk being shifted right out of business.

If there's no transaction velocity in your market and your revenue streams are drying up, *you must look elsewhere*. And competition for the best revenue streams will be fierce.

More importantly, the types of opportunities present in a shift can be complicated, often requiring the involvement of multiple experts before a transaction is actually completed. If you can offer all of the expertise required—a turnkey solution through your own experience and knowledge, through the resources of your brokerage office or through your partnerships with key resources—you will be well-positioned to take advantage of more and higher-quality opportunities and capture more of the available revenue. Offering a single point of contact to potential clients who may be overwhelmed by complexity is an excellent way to differentiate your commercial practice in a shifted market.

The question I'm often asked by commercial brokers challenged by the current shift is, "What opportunities are out there? What should I be doing?" First, follow the advice we've been offering throughout: Expand your knowledge of your market and specialties to identify trends that you can leverage, properties to pursue, and prospects to convert. Knowing which property types are out of favor and what price points will attract motivated buyers will separate you from the less-successful commercial broker in a shifting market.

Second, recognize that in almost any shifted market, the critical lines of business you must grow are as follows:

1. Tenant and landlord leasing representation and property management

2. Turnkey consultation on distressed assets

3. High-quality property sales

The spectacular opportunities of a shift are to expand your knowledge and market reach to develop expertise that you can leverage in any market, and to create growth with the next upswing and stability in the next shift.

1. TENANT AND LANDLORD LEASING REPRESENTATION AND PROPERTY MANAGEMENT

Most of my career in commercial real estate has been in representing tenants. And while shifted markets have never been easy, this base of reliable income has ensured my success through good markets and bad. Why? The answer is in the averages. The term of the average commercial lease, particularly for multitenant properties, is approximately five years; therefore, about 20 percent of leases roll or expire in any given year—whether the market is up or down. While investment sales can vary greatly in transaction volume from market cycle to market cycle, lease transactions are much less volatile. Businesses always need space, landlords always need tenants, and at the very least, leases need to be extended or renegotiated. Consequently, leasing is a steady stream of income in any market, and in a shifted market, it's a bright spot in an otherwise cloudy picture.

CHANGE TO SALES

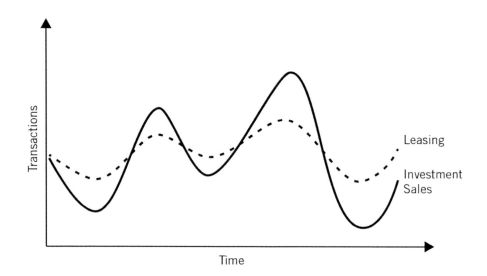

Figure 30 – Cycles of transaction volume volatility are smaller for tenant and landlord representation

Broker services are needed more than ever in a shifted market: Landlords need strategies for attracting and keeping quality tenants, while tenants need help finding the best deal possible. In a shifted market, successful commercial brokers should spend a disproportionate amount of their business development efforts on building their tenant and landlord representation practices.

If you are not already capitalizing on this opportunity, your next move should be to develop expertise in representing both tenants and landlords, building your knowledge of all of the issues they face given the current economic climate, many of which we've discussed earlier.

Tenants in a shifted market need quality representation more than ever. Often, their needs shift right along with the economy—more space, less space, selling a property and moving into leased space, etc.—and they don't realize all of the commercial opportunities available to have their needs met. For many businesses, real estate costs can be the second-largest line item in the expenses on their income statement, so helping a company reduce its real estate costs directly impacts its bottom line. Many tenants just don't realize how much you might be able to help them shift that number on their P&L.

Likewise, they may know that they hold the power, but they don't understand the nuances of the market. They want the best price possible, so it's in their best interest to work with an expert broker rather than trying to work directly with the property management company. And because landlords

Through the advice of my commercial coach, I have formed a strategic alliance with professionals across the country and have focused my business on high quality net-leased investment sales and tenant representation. I have also started building my team and added three juniors—one to assist me with the net-leased assets, one focused on buyer/tenant representation, and one focused on multifamily. Additionally, we continue to pursue and service key bank/ REO relationships I have fostered over the past few years. This positioning of my commercial business has proven to be a very profitable strategy.

Ken Wimberly,
Dallas, Texas

are anxious to fill their spaces, developing knowledge of concessions and other opportunities they are willing to offer will help you serve your tenant clients well.

On the opposite side of the fence, property management for landlords or owners has become a bread-and-butter revenue stream for many brokers. Rhonda West has been in the commercial real estate business since 1979—she's seen shifted markets before. "Property management is needed in good times, and it is *really* needed in bad times," she explains. When Rhonda first opened a new commercial real estate office in Honolulu some years ago, she quickly found that the market was sewn up by other established companies. But then she heard about a potential opportunity on a neighboring island. What she found there was a host of owners of resort and rental properties who were "self-managing." So Rhonda developed a property management business, for which there was almost no competition. And seizing this market of the moment enabled her and her team to become established commercial brokers in Honolulu. Page Aiken, managing director in Atlanta, Georgia, often utilizes property management to establish additional business opportunities with a prospective landlord. "We provide property management services as a way to build a relationship with the owner in order to gain leasing assignments; and leasing assignments, once we are successful, establish investment sales opportunities."

There are obvious synergies between property management and other work brokers do. In fact, in some states, commercial property managers are required to be licensed brokers. If you historically represent tenants, you can leverage your detailed knowledge of the leasing markets to branch into landlord leasing and property management contracts as well. Additionally, you can develop a deep knowledge of the market that can be leveraged in your other work as well, including investment sales. For instance, if you do a feasibility study for an investment client, landlords will understand that you have an intimate knowledge of market rents and property expenses, thus enabling you to convert this knowledge into additional leasing and property management assignments.

You can also offer the knowledge you gain through property management for a fee in the form of consultative services, a tactic Rhonda has used to expand her income streams. "Because we have dual knowledge in property management and investment sales, we are often asked to come in as consultants and do feasibility assessments for a fee—yet another source of income."

Even though all types of transactions and all commissions take a hit in a shifted market, tenant and landlord representation can be two essential sources of reliable commission revenue. In identifying and finding a new location and negotiating for a tenant, Dale Donovan, managing director, Orlando, Florida, finds it extremely beneficial to have tenant representation guidelines and expectations outlined at the outset. "When properly managed, the site selection process can save the client considerable time and money." The step-by-step site selection guidelines are great tools that can be utilized in developing the tenant/broker relationship as well as be a resource throughout the process. "It has proven throughout my career, when you have an informed client and they know what to expect in this process, it leads naturally to a much smoother and successful transaction."

ELEVEN STEPS TO SUCCESSFUL SITE SELECTION

When properly managed, the site selection process can save your client time and money. The following sample process serves to illustrate steps from evaluation through completion.

STEP 1: EVALUATION

Identify and analyze company's needs, timeline, and facility or property requirements.

STEP 2: DETERMINE GEOGRAPHIC PRIORITIES

Analyze geographic areas for strategic positioning.

STEP 3: IDENTIFY AND EVALUATE PROSPECTIVE SITES

Research prospective sites, utilizing clients' requirements and parameters.

STEP 4: TOUR SELECTED SITES

Preview proposed sites identified in step 3. Rank the sites in order of preference. Tour selected sites with client.

STEP 5: PROPOSAL PROCESS

Outline items of importance specific to occupancy and/or build-to-suit. Negotiate with multiple landlords concurrently.

STEP 6: INITIAL SPACE PLANNING

Interface with architects, engineers, and contractors to determine facility requirements and tenant improvements or the development process.

STEP 7: ECONOMIC, MARKET, AND AMENITY ANALYSIS

Prepare economic and amenity analysis relative to each of the proposed sites.

STEP 8: FINAL NEGOTIATIONS

Negotiate lease/purchase details and terms, and coordinate and expedite the execution of final lease/sale documents.

STEP 9: CONSTRUCTION OF IMPROVEMENTS

Ensure improvements are built to client specifications and are on time and on budget. Assist in coordination with landlord.

STEP 10: COMPLETION/CLOSING

Assure that contract obligations are fulfilled to client satisfaction. Coordinate move-in/closing of property management issues as appropriate.

STEP 11: CONFIRM PROJECT DETAILS

Assure that contract obligations are fulfilled to client satisfaction.

Figure 31

2. TURNKEY CONSULTATION ON DISTRESSED ASSETS

In the last tactic, we explained the precarious situation banks face now and in the near future. From 2011 through 2013, approximately $1.2 trillion in commercial loans will come due, according to the Mortgage Brokers Association. The majority of these loans were made at peak or near-peak market valuations, and thus a large percentage have the potential to be distressed or nonperforming. As more and more banks and other lien-holders take back properties or restructure loans, an entirely new class of clientele is emerging—clients in need of your expertise and leadership. There is little doubt that a market of the moment for commercial real estate over the next few years will be to work with banks and asset managers that own or control the loans of these troubled assets.

While distressed assets are common in a shift, the uncommon skills you develop in handling these types of transactions and the client contacts you make can be leveraged long after the market has improved. You are presented with an opportunity to build unique lines of business based on these complex opportunities.

The most important thing to know about dealing with distressed assets is that they can be complicated, thus banks and note holders—who are in the loan-servicing business, not the property ownership or management business—need experts who can simplify the complexity for them, help them understand market conditions affecting the property, and guide them in making sound business decisions. The most valuable way to differentiate yourself is to position your brokerage as a one-stop shop, regardless of what may happen with a property. You must demonstrate to prospective clients at your first meeting that you offer a single point of contact with a service proposition for every potential turning point in the process, either through services you offer in-house or through partnerships with other key service providers.

When working with a note or lienholder—bank asset managers, hard-money lenders, commercial mortgage-backed security trustees—keep their goals in mind: to turn a nonperforming loan into a performing loan or to extract the most value possible from a bad loan and get it out of their portfolio. The process for helping your client down either path is shown in figure 32. Use this graphic the first time you meet with a prospective client and explain the service proposition you bring to the table at each point in the process and for each possible outcome.

Five-Stage Consultation on Distressed Assets
Analysis, Strategic Recommendation, and Servicing

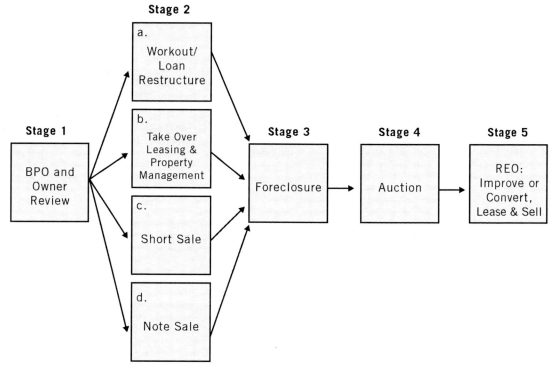

Figure 32

Stage 1

Often, your first role in working with a distressed asset is as a third-party, nonconflicted validator of market facts. Potential service opportunities will come once you conduct a broker price opinion and owner review. This is often done on assets that are showing early signs of nonperformance. You will need to assess each property and the management of it to determine the following:

a. What is a realistic current market price for the property?

b. Is the property a quality property: good location, good tenants if it's lease based, good potential long-term value?

c. Is the property being well-maintained? Will its value improve with the market?

d. If it's a lease property, is the landlord doing all of the right things to improve occupancy and maintain good relationships with current tenants?

Stage 2

Once you've made your assessment in a consultative role, you are in a position to not just simply report your findings, but also to recommend an appropriate course of action. Every property is different; there is no formula for fixing a nonperforming asset. Your recommendations must be based on your critical assessment of the property. Depending on what you find, you'll typically make one of four recommendations:

2a. If the property is quality and stands a good chance of returning to its former value as the market improves, and the owner is doing a good job of maintaining and leasing it, you might recommend that the bank restructure the loan or develop a workout arrangement with the current owner.

2b. For a lease-based property that isn't being managed or leased well, you might recommend that the bank take control of the property management and leasing—handing those services over to your commercial team, of course. This might happen in conjunction with a loan restructure. This situation sets you up to handle the sale of the property if the owner continues to be delinquent on the loan. Don't take over property management or leasing on any property that you have little hope of filling with quality tenants. For those properties, you may have to recommend option 2d below.

2c. A similar option for a high-quality property is a short sale, which allows the bank to replace the current ownership with a new one and restructure the note, often resulting in smaller losses for the bank because they can ensure that a percentage of the outstanding loan amount is covered. This is often the most appealing option for the owner of the property

> *The commercial agent that can provide turnkey services will be the agent of choice. Turnkey means providing all facets of service for the property, from receivership to property management, asset preparation and either leasing or sale of the asset.*
> *Kristan Cole,*
> *Wasilla, Alaska*

as well, who is likely to feel relieved to get out from under a property note without being foreclosed on. And of course, you are well-positioned to handle the short sale for them. This is when your stable of cash buyers makes you invaluable to your banking client.

2d. The bank can also sell the note, bundling it with notes on other properties. While the decision to sell the note will be based almost entirely on the bank's assessment of the asset quality of its portfolio, you may still be able to play a role in that decision, and even in the note sale. If you have connections with hedge funds or cash buyers that might consider buying the notes, you can make the connection between the two institutions. The bank will usually take this option with truly distressed or value-add properties that have little chance of providing a return in the near term without significant investment of capital. That said, they could bundle the poorest-performing notes with notes that are performing—although barely—to raise the price of the entire note pool. All these scenarios involve a substantial discount to the underlying note amount, so make sure the bank is able to take this type of "hit" to their Tier 1 capital. Even notes that are performing but are on a watch list because of late payments are trading at a heavily discounted price. But be assured that most banks would prefer to get these nonperforming notes off the books before their next audit.

And if they do sell the note, you could potentially lose access to that property or you may suddenly have a new client. In the case of a note sale, you'll need to work quickly to prove your value to the new lienholder. And that's easier to do if you already have intimate knowledge of the commercial properties in question.

When you make your recommendation, regardless of what it is, you have to be prepared for the fact that the state of the bank's overall portfolio may heavily influence their decision on the property. The Federal Deposit Insurance Corporation (FDIC) sets limits on the amount of commercial real estate loans a bank can make in relation to its equity or Tier 1 capital position. If the ratio of total commercial real estate loans to Tier 1 capital is 300 percent or higher, the bank is considered to be "CRE concentrated," and the FDIC will put pressure on them to reduce their outstanding loans. However, a bank's Tier 1 capital is also reduced when it *writes down the loan*, so the asset manager may not be interested in moving toward foreclosure or other proactive measures, choosing instead to work with owners even if it's unlikely the loan will begin to perform again.

With the number of loans with assets that have plummeted in value, we may soon see bank closures as a result of the poor asset quality of their commercial loan portfolios. Today's commercial banks are fearful of another crisis like the savings and loan debacle of the 1980s. They are being more cautious, and are clearly afraid or unable to write down the loan losses. This fear has resulted in delays in the decision-making process and is a primary reason

> *Asset managers will always choose the firms with proven abilities in the marketplace. Our goal is to create a "single point of contact" solution by delivering market presence, product knowledge, and brokers and service providers that possess the skill sets needed to manage the complexity of these transactions for our clients. My goal is to never embarrass and always make the asset manager shine. The ability to truly deliver on accountability as well as direct access to the information sources is key to working with distressed asset clientele.*
>
> *Annie Pearl,*
> *Boca Raton, Florida*

for the tremendous downturn in investment sales transaction volume. Select the banks you work with carefully—review key data to ensure that they are able to take the losses that may be necessary. Otherwise, they will be forced to continue the practice of "extend and pretend" and you won't see any transactions.

Tom Daves, of Roseville, California, first learned to work with financial institutions on residential take-backs, and used his contacts at the banks in order to connect with the commercial real estate asset managers. "The banks are willing to work with owners of distressed assets now, in an 'extend and pretend' mode, because they don't want to add more commercial real estate to their portfolios of REO."

Ultimately, restructuring and workouts won't solve many problems. Even if you take over property leasing and management, you may not be able to improve rent rolls enough to cover the cost of operations and the loan. And while it's always preferable to complete a short sale rather than foreclose on a property, short sales don't always come through, particularly on lower-quality properties.

Stage 3

If you see little opportunity for the loan to perform or for other options to produce a better return, you would probably recommend that the bank cut its losses and move directly to a foreclosure.

While you won't likely be involved in the foreclosure proceedings, which can take months or even a year if the company ends up going Chapter 11, if you've positioned yourself correctly, you should be playing an advisory role, helping the asset manager deal with the property once the foreclosure process is complete, moving through the auction process and into REO management.

Stage 4

Generally, the bank will first try to auction the property, possibly more than once. How aggressively they price it for auction will often depend on their debt/equity ratio and capital position. Depending on the age of the original loan and how long it was performing before they were forced to foreclose, they may walk away without taking a total bath. A few brokers who are knowledgeable in this area can take advantage of the opportunity to earn fees by organizing auctions and representing their bank clients. Even if you simply partner with an auction company, you can earn a referral fee. And you may have a hot deal to bring to your cash buyers.

Stage 5

If the bank does not get the price they want through auction, they'll often consider moving the property into their REO portfolio, working with a broker to improve the property or convert it (see Tactic #8), increase occupancy if it's lease based, and sell it on the open market to recoup as much value as possible. This process could take twelve to eighteen months, but if you educate the bank on the quality of the property and its potential, they may be willing to take this path. Again, this is an opportunity for you to manage the conversion, handle the leasing and property management, and handle the sale—generating multiple income streams from a single property by stepping in and playing the role of interim owner.

By teaming up with an auction provider, the local expert will expand the tools they can offer to a lender or client and expand their own business. A lender will feel more confident in listing a property with a broker who has the ability to seamlessly roll a conventional sale into an accelerated one through the commercial auction process.

Mark Raccuia,
Chicago, Illinois

While the process of working with distressed properties can be long and intensive, revenue opportunities exist at every point along the way. You can charge consulting fees from the very beginning, earn steady long-term income if you take over property management and leasing, and earn a commission if you handle the short sale or the sale after foreclosure. And all along the way, you gather market knowledge and skills that you can leverage in every other part of your business.

If you don't already have deep contacts with commercial banks in your area, try these tips for expanding into distressed asset management:

1. Bring them a cash buyer – Leverage your stable of qualified buyers who are interested in distressed assets. Prove your value right from the start.

2. Leverage your residential agent network to get connected through agents that have been assisting banks for years with their residential distressed assets – Len May learned about helping banks with problem assets through a referral from an REO residential agent. "The bank they were working with had one or two commercial properties, and so they brought us in to talk with the asset manager. They needed help with notes disposition. We took this on and developed a new specialty area, which also moved us into asset recovery disposition work. Now we provide strategic consultation (rather than just tactical BPO valuations), including helping them determine an exit strategy for bad notes. We consider all avenues: short sales, pre-foreclosure, sales of the note, deed in lieu of foreclosure, or REO. We also consider how the asset's disposition will affect the bank's

debt/equity ratios and capital positions. We are now a trusted partner, and help them find the right specialists (if not us) to take care of their commercial properties."

3. Become the market leader in the types of properties or geographic areas where distressed assets may be common – While larger national banks will typically utilize existing relationships with national brokerage firms to meet their needs, they may look for a local expert in a specific market, given larger firms rarely have offices covering secondary markets and Tier II cities.

4. Become a court-appointed receiver – Determine if you must be licensed or if you must complete specific training. Being the court-appointed receiver for properties provides you with immediate opportunities (an hourly fee, leasing commissions) and potential to represent the owner or bank when the property is sold. Dan Henderson, of Charleston, South Carolina, has worked with a local bank for many years. He used to do site selection for them and then was asked to be a receiver. He talked to a lawyer, filed the necessary paperwork, and now works with the bank directly to manage their commercial real estate portfolio.

5. Team up with another broker in a noncompeting area or specialty to share introductions or to provide single source solutions – If your specialty is multifamily, team with retail, industrial, and office brokers to deliver a range of services. To provide specialization in a wider geographic area, partner with specialists in other markets. Have each broker make appointments to introduce you to their

local bank asset manager, and then do the same for them. According to Tom Daves, "Banks aren't used to commercial real estate brokers working together. Historically, the commercial real estate world has been cutthroat, with very little cooperation. Commercial brokers are seen as lone wolves. By partnering, we offer managers the benefit of a single point of contact in all areas. We have more resources to offer, and those resources are experts in their local market or in their asset class."

6. Obtain a list of LLC companies in your area that are in Chapter 11 bankruptcy – Use PACER.gov lists and your network to discover if any of the companies listed own properties in your area. Working directly with the owners of potential distressed properties will give you an opportunity to connect with asset managers at banks and with other lenders.

7. Use foreclosure identification services like ForeclosureRadar and lender information resources like *The Lane Guide* to identify properties that are in trouble and the asset managers responsible for them – Contact the banker or asset manager and probe for pain, discover goals and objectives regarding the property, and develop a creative and proactive pathway to achieving those goals.

3. HIGH-QUALITY PROPERTY SALES

It's no surprise that quality properties are a market of the moment during a shift. There is always a flight to quality by the investment community during uncertain times. The difference is that in a shift, it's likely that quality properties—particularly in terms of cash flow and NOI—will be the primary properties being financed, as investors increasingly seek less uncertainty with their investment portfolios.

Andrew Barnes, managing director of the National NNN Investment Group in San Francisco, California, specializes in single-tenant, net-lease real estate. NNN leases, called "triple net" leases, are long-term, hands-off commercial leases. The landlord's income from the property is a net of property taxes, insurance, and common maintenance expenses, all of which are paid for by the tenant. Investors typically purchase triple-net investments because they are selling a management-intensive apartment property as part of a 1031 tax-deferred exchange, or because they are engaged in a forward-looking estate planning strategy. The common objective in purchasing an income-producing triple-net property is to enjoy stable, long-term, passive income.

Andrew noted that "there has been a flight to quality during this shifting market period. The type of investor who flocks to U.S. treasuries is the same investor who is currently fueling demand for 'A plus' credit, triple-net properties." Andrew's Walgreens properties,

The multifamily sector has generally been outperforming all other sectors: people need a place to live, and in the face of foreclosures, they need apartments.

Chuck Frankel,
New York, New York

which have a twenty-five-year primary term, absolute NNN lease, sometimes make him feel like a bond salesman. Investor demand is outstripping supply for these income-producing, high-credit tenant properties. "They are often viewed by more aggressive investors as 'boring,' safe generators of passive income. They rarely provide the opportunity for the owner to add value or receive an appreciation pop upon exit the way a multifamily property might. But in these uncertain times, the investor market cannot get enough of these 'steady Eddie' properties. Additionally, lenders are actively seeking high-credit, triple-net properties to lend on because it gives the lender the opportunity to put money into circulation at what they perceive to be a low risk, balancing the more risky parts of their loan portfolios with more conservative notes."

Other quality yield properties that are likely to attract buyers are class "A" multitenant office and retail properties, medical properties, or multifamily properties that are 90 to 95 percent occupied. Investors know that they will earn a safe return on these. For multifamily properties, as the single-family residential market shifts, fewer people can afford home ownership, thus creating upward pressure on rental and occupancy rates. And hotels and multifamily properties generally are easier to sell because they don't have outdated, long-term leases in place, and so offer more reliable net operating income projections.

A key reason for the availability of buyers for these types of properties is the availability of financing, according to Butch West, a commercial veteran in Austin, Texas. "Multifamily and medical are the primary types of properties that are getting financing right now. Everything else is a crapshoot. For these, you still have to prove strong cash flow for lenders to take an interest."

Eventually, the trends may shift, but these properties are a safe bet for investors because there is manageable and quantifiable risk involved. The return on investment may not be as great as on a value-add property with a more reduced price, but in uncertain times, many investors are simply looking for a safe way to beat the returns on money market funds and to generate reliable cash flow.

Pursue these properties relentlessly, and connect with the investors and sellers who are most likely to be associated with them. Jeffrey Peldon, from Los Angeles, California, states, "We recognized the lack of available funding for typical investment sale properties and have shifted our team's work to focus on multifamily properties and fully leased or single tenant properties. This is where the action is."

We've talked about the importance of shifting your perspective along with shifts in the market in every tactic in this book; however, it may be more important here than in any other. Few people really enjoy and embrace change—it's not in our nature. Even as we watch income levels drop, we tend to cling to what we know, to what feels normal in the face of chaos. Instead, you must focus your attention, resources, efforts, and expertise-building in areas where income is more likely and more consistent. It's the only way to survive a shift and come out stronger on the other side.

TACTIC #12
BULLETPROOF THE TRANSACTION –
ISSUES AND SOLUTIONS

Communication is a skill that you can learn.
It's like riding a bicycle or typing: If you're willing to work at it,
you can rapidly improve the quality of every part of your life.
Brian Tracy

"When people ask me how I got a major motion picture made, I tell them I didn't know I couldn't. I just set my sights on a goal and got it done," says Michael Balson, who produced the action film *Bat*21* with Gene Hackman and Danny Glover in 1988. Michael now applies that same attitude in his work as director of commercial real estate in the Beverly Hills region of California. He applies persistence and intention, a practice that was particularly helpful in closing a recent transaction.

Michael represented a buyer interested in a portfolio of four apartment properties totaling 222 units. However, the properties weren't actually on the market. So the first hurdle was positioning his client as a ready buyer with the owner. "I've lost deals in the past by letting go of a prospect after hearing that they were not interested in selling. What I've learned is that it pays to stay in touch. Sometimes an owner will decide to sell for reasons you don't anticipate, and you want to be who they think of first."

When the owner was ready, so was Michael. But then came the inevitable lending hurdles. The properties were encumbered by CMBS loans of about $20 million, and his client would be required to assume those loans as part of the off-market transaction. And even though his client was imminently qualified, it took months for lenders to hit the ball back, to process the assumption application and related paperwork. Michael called and emailed not only the point person at the bank but also his boss, constantly checking on the status, trying to get the process moving. While it still took months for the lender to approve the transaction, who knows what would have happened if Michael hadn't been so diligent in his efforts on behalf of his client.

In the end, after numerous rounds of negotiations among all the parties, the transaction went through. And even though he was operating in a shifted market, Michael closed the transaction—the biggest of his commercial real estate career at about $40 million.

Closing commercial transactions in today's shifted market requires a close, consistent eye on every transaction element throughout the process. At any point, any seemingly innocuous detail could quickly become the downfall of the entire transaction. You could say this is true in most markets, but in a shift it can define every deal in your pipeline if you aren't exceedingly cautious. You can't afford to lose even one transaction because of a miscommunication or misunderstanding.

The old mantra of "time kills deals" is never more true than now, and the current state of the market is prolonging most transactions. Due diligence periods that used to

Getting timely and accurate information is critical to closing transactions in a shifting marketplace, and I have developed a great relationship with my local title company representative to gain this competitive advantage. I chose Stewart Title because they are national in scope and have a great reputation.

Butch West,
Austin, Texas

be 60 to 90 days are now 180 days or more. Appraisers, environmental consultants, and other professionals are taking longer to issue reports; nobody wants to put their name next to a number that may change before the transaction is complete. Thus it is imperative for the successful commercial broker to anticipate problems and ensure that all parties have the information they need to move forward.

If you want to get paid, you have to ensure that no details are lost, that no party in a transaction goes dark, that nothing gets in the way of the transaction's momentum. Once you lose momentum, you've likely lost the deal—and the commission.

To ensure this doesn't happen and you get paid:

1. Pursue only viable transactions

2. Be systematically proactive

3. Align interests to solve problems

4. Avoid the "commission-ectomy"

And always remember two realities of the shift. First, this is primarily a singles market—don't always swing for the fences. Remember the top investment sales broker whose commission income was down more than 90 percent! Fill your pipeline with multiple smaller and mid-level transactions to account for the higher fallout ratio—don't rely on one single large transaction to make your year. And second, presume most prospects will waste your time and resources on nonproductive, noncommissionable work. As a commercial broker, your time is a valuable, limited commodity, and thus it must be guarded and protected for viable transaction business clientele.

1. PURSUE ONLY VIABLE TRANSACTIONS

When times are tough, the tough who make it through are persistent, focused, and solutions oriented. These are critical skills in a shift. But if you aren't careful, they are also the attributes that can drive you to waste time on transactions that will never close.

"There's an old saying: A drowning man will grasp at straws," said Cliff Bogart. Brokers in a shift may grasp at any transaction, ignoring obvious signs that it is problematic. They waste time chasing deals that will never generate income. Cliff's solution to these tendencies? "The only remedy is to work smart, try not to react emotionally, and try to evaluate transactions as honestly as possible. The more you can perceive potential problems before they occur and qualify transactions early, the less time you'll waste working transactions that will never close." Recall the story I told in Tactic #2 of the broker I worked with who would review every transaction in my pipeline and rate its chances of completing. Having a coach to help you through this analysis can be invaluable.

We discussed the importance of qualifying buyers in a shifted market in Tactic #5. That same clear-eyed approach should be used throughout the transaction. Cliff recommends the following tactics:

1. Discover the obstacles up front by asking questions about any aspect of the property or the transaction that you think could create difficulties down the line. Get very clear on these hurdles and whether they will prevent a transaction from completing. Less-experienced brokers should talk to more experienced ones to get advice about how to manage these problems or to get a realistic assessment of whether they are solvable.

2. Just as we told you to set clear expectations with your clients, be frank with potential buyers or tenants about price and financing. For instance, if the owner isn't willing to budge on price or isn't willing to consider owner financing, tell the buyer the truth of that situation. Say, "If you don't have your financing in order, this probably isn't the property for you." In a shifting market, buyers and tenants are demanding more than the normal amount of concessions and contingencies. If any concessions are off the table for your seller, be sure to communicate those early on. And if any contingencies are an absolute requirement for your investor or tenant, do the same.

3. Qualify buyers, sellers, landlords, and tenants in terms of the usual factors—motivation, urgency, funding—but also in terms of the potential difficulties of that particular property or transaction. Get it out up front so that you don't waste anybody's time.

My commercial coach, Reagan Dixon, has helped me with accountability in my core competencies. It helped me see what my strengths are and what I need to be spending most of my time on. I am on track to have a very profitable year by going back to the key activities that drive lead generation and lead conversion.

Michelle Rich,
Raleigh, North Carolina

Having said that, in better times when pipelines are full, brokers sometimes have the luxury of passing on smaller opportunities because there are too many problems to solve in relation to the income potential. In a shift, there are numerous mid-level and smaller opportunities—real transactions—that a broker might have otherwise overlooked but they should now pursue. Just because a transaction requires more work doesn't mean it won't pay out—as long as the parties to the transaction understand what the issues are and are prepared to work together to solve them.

2. BE SYSTEMATICALLY PROACTIVE

In a shift, the moment you assume smooth sailing is the moment the skies turn dark and the wind blows you over. The only way to ensure that doesn't happen is to keep your eye on your lines, track the wind, and scan the horizon. Assume nothing! You must be proactive at every stage of the transaction, from setting clear expectations when you sign a listing or representation agreement with a client to being actively involved with appraisals and inspections to ensuring that every party views the transaction as a success after the contracts are signed. As we've discussed in other tactics, you need to be a one-stop shop of expertise, and even in the final moments before closing, you can't assume that the deal is done. A contract pending today means that there's maybe a 50 percent chance of a closed transaction, not 90 percent. The best way to ensure the survival of a transaction is keep the boat headed in the right direction and avoid surprise gales.

The downfall of most transactions is lack of a proactive system to support free-flowing communication. Most brokers today still rely on hard copies of contracts and other paperwork, using couriers to run papers all over town to get signatures every time one party makes an adjustment to a contract, losing days to the review of each form or addendum, and generally slowing the momentum of the transaction. It's inefficient at best, and it often leaves you in the dark as problems arise—until it's too late to solve them.

Imagine handling a portfolio of hundreds of properties totaling more than 5 million square feet of space. For most brokers, it probably sounds like a dream come true or completely overwhelming—or both. In 2006, the company I was with decided to pursue a commercial brokerage services contract with the county of San Diego to handle all of their commercial needs for just such a portfolio. The sheer number of transactions involved was mind-boggling. Worse, though, was the bureaucratic red tape required to complete each transaction, the number of people who would be party to every decision, the number of signatures required for each lease agreement, the cacophony of minute details. If you've ever worked with a government entity, you understand the potential magnitude of the problem. If we weren't careful, we'd lose many transactions due to lack of communication, or lose money on every transaction just paying for gas driving from office to office to get signatures. We needed a system for keeping everybody informed, for ensuring that all of the details were captured and communicated, and for streamlining the process. We needed to bulletproof every transaction.

Given the economic uncertainties clients are facing in these challenging times, one of the most critical steps necessary, prior to acquiring or leasing commercial real estate for operational purposes, is a comprehensive transaction management process. To successfully address these challenges, commercial real estate brokers must change their business model from one of pure sales to include more advisory activities. This transformation will make them more valuable to their client and give them a pivotal role to play in supporting wider organizational objectives in mergers and acquisitions.

Ray Meglio,
New York, New York

We approached the county officials with a brokerage services plan with an online and secure transaction management system that would allow us to keep all parties informed on the progress and details of each transaction assignment. Without that system, it's unlikely that we would have been able to effectively capture or service a client with such a massive property portfolio.

We discussed the powerful leverage an online transaction management system (TMS) can offer in Tactic #3. In a shift, when trying to bulletproof every transaction, it's the best tool at your disposal. It will dramatically reduce the time it takes to get approvals, it makes communicating new information simple and effective, and it ensures that every party in the transaction has all of the same information and is on the same page. Think of a TMS as an online file cabinet that lets you share all of the electronic documents related to a transaction securely and confidentially with all of the parties to that transaction.

Use the Internet to communicate with clients. Do online red-lining of documents. It's much more effective to do this using a collaborative document sharing system.
Charles "Mac" McClure,
Dallas, Texas

A good TMS will help you track versions and may even alert everybody with access to the documents each time somebody makes changes. Many will also allow you to create timelines with deadline alerts, network with other brokers or other specialists you may need as part of the transaction, generate real-time reports, and even allow for virtual signatures to ensure that no document is incomplete at the end of a transaction.

And as a senior broker, it can help you ensure that transactions being managed by junior brokers aren't falling apart. "I've gone in and salvaged projects, because there's no lag—it doesn't take days to uncover a problem," said Steven McMurtrie, director of commercial sales offices in northern California. As mentioned in Tactic #3, he reviews all transactions once a week, quickly and effectively. And it has helped him secure clients too. "We got a call from a potential client in Los Angeles. They were interviewing brokers, but as they met with other brokers in our company, I was emailing them to explain that they would also be getting my leadership and the support of our commercial operations manager on every transaction."

This is how you keep the momentum of a transaction moving forward right from the start; delays over minor issues are how you lose momentum. There are a host of TMS tools available now, some specifically designed for real estate professionals and some that you might have to adapt to your needs. Seek them out and put them to use.

If a TMS isn't right for you at this time, create your own system to ensure that, at every step in the process, you know how the transaction is doing, you are communicating all relevant details, and you have all of the approvals you need. A great personal tool is the simple checklist. In *The Checklist Manifesto*, Atul Gawande tells a story that communicates the power of a checklist. In October of 1935, the U.S. Army Air Corps was performing flight competitions among airplane manufacturers for the next long-range bomber. The Boeing model had been outperforming all other planes in early evaluations, and these test flights were considered to be a simple formality before the U.S. Army Accessions Command signed off on an order for sixty-five planes.

Army brass and executives watched as the plane taxied down the runway, "roared down the tarmac, lifted off smoothly, and climbed sharply to 300 feet. Then it stalled, turned on one wing, and crashed in a fiery explosion. Two of the five crew members died, including the pilot."

All in attendance were horrified, of course, but they were also dumbfounded. What could have happened? As the investigation unfolded, they discovered that, mechanically, the plane had been sound. Initially, the Army went with another design, but some remained convinced that the Boeing plane was better and ordered a few for further testing. What they uncovered was that this new class of airplanes was far more complex than previous aircrafts, and even the most experienced pilots couldn't be expected to remember every detail of getting the plane into the air safely. So they developed a pilot's checklist—the first of its kind—that included every single step, even the most obvious. And that checklist saved the Boeing model 299, which the Army eventually flew 1.8 million miles with no accidents, dubbed the B-17, and was critical to the Allied success in World War II.

Take a lesson from the pilot teams in 1935. Even if you believe you know how to complete every step of the commercial transaction, a comprehensive checklist will help you ensure that you don't get close to a completed transaction and then crash and burn because one small detail was overlooked or one approval was outstanding. You can even tie your checklist to your calendar to develop reminders and alerts at key points in the process. The important thing is to find a way to make sure that no detail is being overlooked.

TRANSACTION MANAGEMENT AND INFORMATION PROCESS

1. PRELIMINARY STAGE

☐ Ascertain the parties' motivations for making the sale and purchase.

☐ Review the parties' valuation of the property to be sold or purchased and examine whether additional consideration needs to be given to this matter.

☐ Review the terms of any proposed broker or finder agreement.

☐ Consider whether a confidentiality agreement is required to protect the parties and their trade secrets during preliminary negotiations.

☐ Consider the appropriate form for the property sale, asset sale, ownership interest sale, merger, etc.

☐ Consider the tax aspects of the transaction.

☐ Consider alternative means of payment of the purchase price, such as allocation of price to covenants not to compete or consulting agreements.

☐ Set up files proposed for the transaction.

2. DUE DILIGENCE INVESTIGATION OF SELLER'S PROPERTY

2.1   RECORDS

☐ Verify that the seller is duly incorporated and in good standing in the state of its incorporation.

☐ Review the articles of incorporation and bylaws of the seller and any amendments.

☐ Determine who are the registered owners of the issued and outstanding shares.

☐ Determine whether there are options, warrants, or other rights to acquire shares outstanding.

☐ Review all agreements between the seller and his/her shareholders.

2.2   PERSONAL PROPERTY

☐ Obtain a list of all machinery, equipment, furniture, and fixtures owned or leased by the seller and depreciation schedules and leases.

☐ Obtain a search of appropriate state and local records for Uniform Commercial Code financing statements and other evidence of liens or encumbrances on the personal property of the seller.

☐ Review the seller's insurance coverage on personal property.

2.3 REAL PROPERTY

☐ Obtain legal descriptions and information about the location and character of all interests in real property owned or leased by the seller.

☐ Review the seller's title insurance policies and consider the purchaser's need for title insurance.

☐ Obtain copies of and review all appraisals of the seller's real property.

☐ Obtain copies of all studies, site evaluations, and governmental filings and reports prepared by consultants or employees of the seller concerning the real property.

☐ Review the seller's real property depreciation schedules.

☐ Review copies of all leases, including amendments, and investigate whether there are any defaults under the leases.

☐ Investigate the presence of hazardous materials or toxic substances on, under, or about any property owned or leased by the seller.

☐ Review insurance coverage.

2.4 FINANCIAL AND TAX INFORMATION

☐ Review the financial statements of the seller for the current year and the past five years.

☐ Review all bank loan agreements.

☐ Obtain copies of property tax assessments for the past five years.

2.5 LEGAL COMPLIANCE AND LITIGATION MATTERS

☐ Determine whether the purchaser can obtain all necessary licenses and permits by transfer from the seller or otherwise.

☐ Review all regulatory reports filed by the seller with governmental agencies within the past five years.

3. LETTER OF INTENT

☐ Prepare a letter of intent after a preliminary decision has been made by the parties to proceed with the sale, and have the letter of intent signed by the parties.

☐ Determine to what extent the letter of intent is going to be binding and on whom.

☐ Prepare timetable, list of responsibilities, and closing memorandum.

4. PURCHASE AGREEMENT

4.1 PRELIMINARY MATTERS

Identification of parties:

☐ Names

☐ Addresses

☐ State or states of incorporation

4.2 ASSETS AND LIABILITIES SUBJECT TO AGREEMENT

Assets subject to agreement:

☐ Business building and other real property

☐ Equipment, furniture, and fixtures

☐ Insurance policies

☐ Other assets

Liabilities subject to agreement:

☐ Contracts

☐ Other liabilities

4.3 PURCHASE PRICE AND PAYMENT TERMS

Amount of consideration:

☐ Single sum

☐ Aggregate of separate sums allocated to various properties and assets

Nature of consideration:

- ☐ Payment of money
- ☐ Other consideration

Allocation of purchase price to various assets sold:

Time and manner of payment:

- ☐ All cash on closing
- ☐ Part payment on signing and balance on closing
- ☐ Deposit held in escrow until closing
- ☐ Installment payments
- ☐ Mortgage or other collateral security
- ☐ Forfeiture of deposit for default in paying purchase price
- ☐ Other methods of payment
- ☐ Personal guaranty of payment by buyer

4.4   CLOSING CONDITIONS AND PROCEDURES

Closing conditions:

- ☐ Verify date and location of closing
- ☐ Consent of shareholders/owners and/or directors/managers
- ☐ Tax rulings
- ☐ Approval by counsel or accountants or both
- ☐ Compliance with UCC Article 6 or other bulk transfer provisions

Closing deliveries:

- ☐ Delivery of instruments of transfer (bill of sale, warranty deed, etc.)
- ☐ Payment of purchase price
- ☐ Estoppel certificates from named organizations

4.5 REPRESENTATIONS AND WARRANTIES

Representations by seller:

☐ Authorization of sale

☐ All outstanding liens, contracts, judgments, and other obligations disclosed

☐ Title to property and assets

☐ Care and preservation of property and assets

☐ Compliance with all laws affecting property

☐ Survival of representations

Representations by buyer:

☐ Corporation validly organized and in good standing

☐ Authorization of acquisition by directors and by shareholders

☐ Other representations

4.6 INDEMNIFICATION OF BUYER

☐ Events or actions triggering indemnification

☐ Escrow requirements

4.7 DEFAULTS AND TERMINATION

☐ Events constituting default

☐ Notice and cure requirements

☐ Remedies and penalties

☐ Other events triggering termination of purchase agreement

5. POSTCLOSING ACTIONS

☐ Record security interests.

☐ Arrange for the creation of any escrows that may be required.

☐ Implement procedures for postclosing adjustment of purchase price, if required.

☐ Pay broker's commission.

☐ Organize documents.

6. CONTACT INFORMATION
☐ Buyer:

☐ Buyer's counsel:

☐ Buyer's accountant:

☐ Buyer's financial adviser:

☐ Seller:

☐ Seller's counsel:

☐ Seller's accountant:

☐ Seller's financial adviser:

Other Contacts:

☐ Regulatory bodies

☐ Lienholders

☐ Other parties from whom consents or approvals are required

Figure 33: You can download a copy of this checklist at www.KellerInk.com/SHIFTCommercial.

Regardless of the technique you use, be active in every aspect of the transaction or else an unknown variable could surface and kill the deal.

3. ALIGN INTERESTS TO SOLVE PROBLEMS

In a shifted market, your buyers and sellers will be exceedingly cautious, the appraiser is not your friend because comparable sales are almost meaningless, inspectors are more concerned about litigation, and lenders have much tighter lending standards. Despite all of your hard work, a transaction can begin to unravel at any time. The more work you put in up front, the less likely this is to happen, but when it does, you need to be ready to leap into problem-solving mode.

First, keep an eye out for any signs that a problem is brewing. Use the rational-man theory: When a transaction is going the way it should go, everyone will behave rationally. Therefore, when anything irrational happens—if someone goes quiet, becomes nonresponsive, is avoiding your calls, has a strange tone of voice—you can be sure there's a reason, and you need to know what it is immediately. If you discover the issue too late, the deal may have already blown up. If there's bad news, you want to get to it as quickly as possible. So don't just call them—set up an appointment or go to their office and camp out on their doorstep until they see you. Don't be afraid to ask them the tough questions. Explain that if you have all of the information, you can most likely offer a remedy to the issue. *Be professionally tenacious*.

Second, once you understand the problem, make sure all parties who should know about it do know about it. Don't brush anything under the rug; it will all come out eventually. If everybody is informed early on, the chances of finding a mutually agreeable solution are much higher. That said, be careful about sharing information before you've fully verified it. There is no point in sending anybody into a panic over a nonissue.

Third, remember that part of a commercial broker's role is to align interests between buyers and sellers or between landlords and tenants. It's just that in a shifted market you will have to dig a little deeper to determine what those interests really are. Cliff Bogart explained that brokers "have to look beyond the positions that various parties take on particular issues. Find the reasoning behind the position. Once you understand the reasoning, you may be able to find a different solution that still meets the actual need." So ask all parties what they really need and then listen carefully for the truth in the answer. Remember the story of creative financing from Chris Sands in Tactic #10: If he didn't know what each party really wanted, the transaction would have fallen apart. And as you seek solutions, keep all parties focused on the core reasons they are at the table. Review Tactic #9 for the best ways to overcome reluctance. Help everybody focus on the big picture issues rather than the smaller variables affecting the transaction. On every occasion, remind them of their core interests to keep them front of mind.

> *As a broker, you have to be totally involved in the transaction and make sure that all terms of the contracts are being met by all parties.*
>
> *Rhonda West,*
> *Austin, Texas*

There are many facets of a transaction that are beyond your control. But brokers are problem solvers, negotiators, and mediators. In a normalized market, a transaction may die once or twice; in a shift, count on it dying many more times. A strong commercial broker instinctively knows how to resuscitate a transaction. Rely on that skill set to approach every problem with a solution-oriented attitude and help find the win-win that will keep the transaction on course.

4. AVOID THE "COMMISSION-ECTOMY"

I can't tell you how many calls I get from brokers complaining that clients aren't paying them the commissions they believe they've earned. In fairness to our esteemed clients, it's not necessarily because they are trying to shirk their bills: In a shifted market, clients may be financially unprepared for all of the aspects of a transaction. Or they may have been prepared, but in the time it takes to complete a transaction, their financial situations may have shifted. Or, the broker may not have communicated the fees or commissions effectively.

Surprisingly, there are simple steps that any broker can take to ensure that they earn the income they deserve on every transaction. Yet even veteran brokers make rookie mistakes by abandoning the basics. Use these proactive tactics to effectively communicate with clients and to forge mutually beneficial and professional relationships.

1. Before you begin to negotiate on the behalf of a client, you must first negotiate on your own behalf. While we absolutely advocate helping clients and providing exceptional service, it is also in everyone's best interest to be up front about the fact that you are not a nonprofit organization—you need to be paid for your valuable knowledge and expertise either through consulting fees or commissions. If your client won't agree to your commission structure up front and in writing, it may be better to move on to other clients.

2. Too many commercial brokers are fearful about speaking candidly with their clients about the commission dollars because the fees can be perceived as high. This is a huge mistake. Your clients will take those fees into account as they are planning the financials of

each transaction and weigh that against your perceived value to the assignment. Don't leave them in the dark and don't set yourself up for a "commission-ectomy" at a later date.

3. Get all fee agreements *in writing*! Signed agreements ensure that everybody is clear on the nature of your commission or fee. Set out the terms, conditions, and services you will provide to your client and how you are to be paid. You are a commercial brokerage professional and should work as such. Make your commission or fee agreement simple and clearly outline how you will earn your payment. Additionally, recall from Tactic #5 that I suggested to include a statement in the agreement that would allow the client to access the commission if they are dissatisfied with your performance—proof positive in your confidence and ability to add value to the transaction.

4. In the shifted market, some commercial brokers are changing from a traditional, transaction-based commission model to a consulting fee arrangement. Be creative in your compensation model. Work out a win-win to ensure your payment motivations align with your client's best interests, which is your ultimate fiduciary duty. For example, you could establish a fee schedule for the better you perform, the more money your client makes, or the faster the building leases up, the higher your brokerage compensation could be.

5. Leverage any other tools you need to protect your business. Get everything in writing, and don't fall victim to the trap of assumptions. Use your full arsenal of commercial brokerage documentation to ensure you get paid, including engagement agreements, listing

agreements, commission agreements, nondisclosure agreements, purchase and sale documents, letters of intent (LOIs), and lease documents.

Follow these fundamentals and you'll avoid the dreaded last-minute "commission-ectomy." Once a deal is underway, it is imperative to keep a constant finger on the pulse of the transaction. A shifted market means that your attention will need to be focused on all aspects of the transaction, through and even after closing. Be sure you're working a viable transaction, make communication clear and consistent, get everything in writing, and be prepared to offer creative solutions to problems that arise. Do whatever is necessary—and legal and ethical—to keep transactions intact and moving forward.

SHIFT INTO ACTION

Success never comes to the chosen few, but the few who choose. These can be the worst of times; these can be the best of times. You get to choose.
GARY KELLER, FROM *SHIFT*

Not long after I began my career in commercial real estate, I decided to leverage what I had learned and try my hand at a different type of brokerage. In many ways, the skill sets and motivations of the two were the same. Becoming an investment broker seemed like an opportunity to try something new, something exciting. And hey, Wall Street brokers seem to have a certain swagger—at least in movies.

Instead, what I discovered is how much I truly enjoy commercial real estate. Yes, many of the skill sets were the same, and to be honest, working for an investment brokerage is where I really honed my cold-calling technique. But for me, nothing is as satisfying as working with owners and investors, tenants, and landlords to negotiate win-win solutions. So approximately six years after leaving the commercial real estate industry, I called my former boss and asked if he could find a place for me again. He opened his doors to me, thank goodness, and I've never looked back.

If you feel the same way about commercial real estate, if it gets your blood pumping in the morning, if you can't wait for your next call with a client or a prospect, if you love what you do and enjoy the rewards it offers, you have no choice but to follow the advice in this book. You can't let a shift keep you from your chosen profession, from exercising the expertise you've developed, and from success in your brokerage practice.

You have to dig deep and find the drive and the wherewithal to make it through. John F. Kennedy said it best: "There are risks and costs to a program of action, but they are far less than the long-range risks and costs of comfortable inaction." No matter how successful you've been, taking the path of comfortable inaction through a shift will surely lead to a diminished career.

Other than offering words of encouragement and thoughts on a shift-survival mindset in Tactic #1, I can't create drive and desire in you. I can't force you to choose success. It's on you to put in the effort required, to choose a *massive action* approach. But what I sincerely hope you have found in these pages is practical tips and techniques that will help you focus your efforts—that will help you earn while others succumb to market churn. By showing you a path through a shifted market, I offer hope that may help you get past the market doldrums to take action today.

Which brings us back to the message of Tactic #1: You must adopt the right mindset in order to take appropriate action. From there, the most important thing you can do is improve your P&L *today* by controlling your expenses, the focus of Tactic #2. Tactic #3 explores the flip side of expenses—leveraging your current resources (both systems and teams) to be as productive as possible by focusing your team on what should be your number one priority: *business development*.

Because business development is the heart of your practice, Tactics #4 through #6 are the heart of the book. In them, we explore how to focus your prospecting, conversion, and online marketing efforts. These tactics are essential, because if you are not pushing your team to expand your business development avenues, you'll come out of the shift weaker rather than stronger. These tactics might hold some of the most important lessons of the book.

Once you have clients to represent and listings to bring to the market, you must find ways to make transactions happen, combating an array of shift-specific obstacles. The first is pricing properties and lease spaces tight to the market, which we cover in Tactic #7. Next, you have to make properties as appealing as possible by focusing on flexibility, as we discuss in Tactic #8. In Tactic #9, we offer advice for helping buyers and tenants get past their hesitancy, their fear, and their belief that somewhere there's a better deal to be had. And Tactic #10 explores the nonconventional sources of funding so that you can advise your clients appropriately and make sure a deal doesn't fall through because of poor credit and capital conditions.

In Tactics #11 and #12, we explore the all-important topic of how to maximize your income in a shifted market. First by expanding your expertise to capitalize on markets of the moment, and then by bulletproofing every transaction to combat the higher rate of deal fallout in a shift, a situation that can eat away at your earning potential if you don't protect your time and your commissions.

Throughout these tactics, we've told stories of other brokers who aren't just scraping by in a shifted market—they're thriving. Those individuals will come out of the shift as market leaders. They are pursuing smart, strategic action and they're driven to take advantage of any opportunities the market presents, no matter how few and far between they might be.

Famed writer and allegorist Gilbert K. Chesterton once wrote, "How you think when you lose determines how long it will be until you win." And I would take that notion further to say that it also determines *how much* you will win. That must be your takeaway. A shifted market does not have to foretell your doom; instead, it can herald in a new stage of your commercial practice—it can be the impetus you need to do what is necessary to capture market share. Seize this opportunity today and use it to leverage the future of your broker practice.

Go out and get your unfair share!